ISLAND DREAMS

Other Works by the Author

How to Love a Goddess, in **The Mystery of Woman, A Book for Men**, edited by Gabriel Morris (2012)

When Santa Cruz Was Young, short story published in **Santa Cruz Weird**, edited by Nancy Lynn Jarvis (2019)

ISLAND DREAMS

A Young Woman's Solo Journey to New Zealand & the South Seas

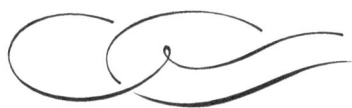

Pamela Morgan

River Sanctuary
PUBLISHING

Island Dreams

ISBN 978-1-952194-14-6

Design by River Sanctuary Graphic Arts
Printed in the United States of America

Additional copies available from:

www.riversanctuarypublishing.com
amazon.com

River Sanctuary Publishing
P.O Box 1561
Felton, CA 95018
www.riversanctuarypublishing.com
Dedicated to the awakening of the New Earth

INTRODUCTION

This journey took place in 1986 – my journal entries provided the foundation for these tales. Yet, the telling of my experiences doesn't come close to capturing the depth of the elusive moments themselves. One could say that all adventures are spiritual, because all journeys involve a leap of faith – not knowing for certain where the path might actually lead us. In the act of moving from one place to another, space is created where moments of self-clarity reveal themselves. Traveling to distant places has a way of opening us, to possibility, to strangeness and events that change us, through which somehow we become more of who we are meant to be.

The guidebook, *Lonely Planet* for budget travelers was my main source of information as to where to go, but recommendations from acquaintances were always an added bonus. Imagine a time when reservations were unnecessary (before Internet), as well as a time when there were four billion fewer people on the planet. We have populated the farthest corners of the planet now – so that today's travelers often find that "paradise" is no longer remote, vacant of tourism, or preserved in its natural state. I feel very fortunate to have taken this trip when I did, allowing me to experience a time in history when life operated on a cosmically slower pace.

An important part of my journey was the people I met along the way. I found that traveling solo and in an unlimited fashion, allowed the TRIP TO TAKE ME with spontaneity and space for wonder to emerge. I counted eleven islands I explored in a period of three months. This was a once-in-a-lifetime experience that can never be repeated, as too much has changed in our world. But I still believe there is magic to discover.

As our memories slowly fade, it becomes important to put our stories down on paper or in video, to remind ourselves that we live in amazing times! By sharing this journey with others, it becomes vivid and can be lived again. I hope that these travels will prove to be an inspiration to young women or anyone desiring to stretch their heart and minds.

September, 2021 Pamela Morgan

PROLOGUE

Fighting back waves of anxiety, my body lifted into another dimension as if floating in slow motion backwards to the exact moment of offense. The next punch to the gut was surprise! My fear took charge, then strangled me of any clear thought of what to do next. *Oh, shit! Where's my passport? Loss of monies is one thing, but my passport?!* The floor fell out from below and tears slowly welled in my eyes, despite holding a stiff upper jaw. I had barely arrived in a city of one million Kiwis – where everything was unfamiliar and foreign. I was alone, truly alone, on the premier morning of my long awaited trip.

All I could do was shamelessly walk to the front desk to report my missing wallet. Since International Youth Hostel (IYH) curfew rules expect guests to leave their accommodations by ten o'clock each morning, I walked outside with a heavy sigh. I stepped painstakingly down each step and then aimlessly wandered nowhere in particular, carrying a pounding hangover and my deflated dignity.

I calmly considered my predicament – I was seven thousand miles from home, alone in a city, on the first day of adventure! I had planned and saved money for this sojourn for a whole year, but at this moment I was destitute. I was only one night away from homelessness in a foreign land with no money!

The whimsical fantasy that I had envisioned years earlier included exploring the unspoiled coastlines of New Zealand and remote South Sea Islands; so far, it was not what the brochures had said it would be. Thief, robbery and an encroaching city skyline were not in any of my imaginings. How many years had I leafed through travel magazines and *National Geographic* dreaming of those mysterious beaches that I could only visit vicariously through a photographer's lens?

Now, HERE I WAS with my tail between my legs, thinking of returning home with a sense of failure, knowing how homeless people might feel with no family, no friends and NO money! At that moment, I didn't even have a name and NO identification to prove who I was! With the best bemused humor I could muster, I told myself . . . I guess I could be AANNNYBODY I wanted to be! I could go anywhere, if I was somebody else, right? Who would that be? Maybe a famous actress? Goldie Hawn? I certainly had her short haircut. Martha Stewart? She was becoming a household name. Maybe a groupie with the Dire Straits band? You name it! How many times in your life do you get the opportunity to create a character from your suppressed imagination? What outlandish situations might unfold if I were to use a new identity to introduce myself? No one would know otherwise . . .

PART ONE

Chapter 1

Some observers might think you're out on a limb. You're pushing the boundaries, hanging out at the frontiers and reinventing your fortune. Long distance contact is filling the gaps in your emotional education. The mountaintop perspective is allowing you to break out of the trance. Go wherever the ideas are most surprising.

Gemini Horoscope at time of departure

It does not seem possible to travel through multiple time zones and arrive two days after you left following an overnight flight. It's like a day was taken away as I vaporized across the international date line. I had actually been in the air over fifteen hours, to be exact, and I was still caught in the thermals of air and space high above the Pacific. I had jetted through Hawaiian and Fijian fuel stops and then was magically rematerialized in an opposing hemisphere called the North Island of New Zealand. During the flight, I had anxiously chatted with a few other vaporized folks while drinking rum and cokes. Other times I tried to nap, but found myself too excited and nervous about the prospects of starting this journey alone, so far away.

On that crisp January morning, I was lifted out of the San Francisco Bay with dew drops in my eyes, as my plane turned and ascended away from my home. The Quantas Boeing arched over the bay and I could see the sparkling waters below the great Golden Gate. All of a sudden my perspective became crystal clear as to everything I was leaving behind! The towering Transamerica and Embarcado buildings had never looked so global, as my family and friends faded into the past.

In a state of jet lag and sleep deprivation, my first evening in Auckland was spent dining across the table from Bert, whom I'd met on the plane. Bert was a bit older – wiry with an athletic build and a Manhattan-edge to his speech and formality. It seemed our adventurous spirits had connected on the plane.

Bert had unexpectedly shown up shortly after I got settled at the budget IYH and invited me out for dinner. He told me he had led Sierra Club hikes to New Zealand before so he was familiar with the city and, by way of introduction, decided to show me around. We walked down towards the waterfront ferry building to the Union Fish Company Restaurant. We shared a bottle of wine while Bert regaled me with stories of some of his hikes in New Zealand, Arizona, Colorado and Utah. He was so educated and worldly compared to my naive untraveled self. His stories brought excitement and inspiration to the joy of travel. How easily we laughed as I toasted and celebrated my newfound freedom. It was a memorable first evening as we dined on raw oysters and local green-lipped mussel fettuccini.

After dinner, Bert and I strolled through the streets in the warm night air. Still feeling out of place, I tried to pass people on the wrong side (pedestrians walk on the left, similar to their custom of driving). Bert grabbed me by the arm several times to avoid colliding and took me to his favorite Auckland pub where we drank Long Island iced teas and danced until closing. At some time after midnight, Bert kindly escorted me woozily back to my hostel. What a gentleman he'd been, graciously offering my first introduction to Auckland and making sure I had arrived safely back to my dorm. I thanked him for a wonderful evening; we hugged and wished each other, "*Happy trails.*"

Next morning's hangover hit hard, like I'd been smacked upside my head! Burdened with pain and heaviness, my head drooped and pounded with every heartbeat. Not wanting to speak to anybody, I sluggishly wandered to the kitchen to make a bowl of muesli. Whatever happened, I may never know. *Did I leave my wallet exposed on the top of my unzipped daypack when I headed to the kitchen to wash my bowl? Did another guest, actually, lift my wallet with all my cash, charge card and traveler's checks? WTF!* I hurried back to my dorm to see if I'd left it behind in my full backpack. Nada, nothing!

After exiting the hostel, I stumbled along crosswalk after crosswalk with no direction until I spotted an alluring provincial park and proceeded toward the big banyan tree surrounded by a cool lawn. I laid my aching head down with a sense of failure and sadness and fell into a deep sleep. Only in slumber could I forget the nightmare of my reality.

I awoke several hours later still burdened with my predicament, but knowing that my stolen identity was my karmic "gotcha" somehow. At that moment, I calmly checked my pockets: Wow, I had ninety-three cents in shiny New Zealand coins! It was a Sunday and everything from convenience stores to pubs were closed by law. My thoughts seemed to swirl in a useless vortex of shame and worry.

It will always remain one of the most hideous days of my life, but a ray of hope came that evening while sitting at the community dining tables back at the hostel. As I shared my sad story with another traveler, low and behold, my traveling "angel" appeared and shared some of her dinner, then loaned me twenty dollars! Graciousness accepted!

Throughout the interminable evening, I fretted and replayed in my head how lame I had been to have lost my wallet so quickly, followed by a littany of worry: *will the bank be able to reissue my traveler's checks without any form of identification? Can I continue this trip without a credit card?*

How recklessly celebratory I had been to drink so much that first night with Bert. But the painful lesson quickly woke me up from naively trusting others while staying in international city hostels. My belief in a benevolent reality gave way to a more balanced caution. Sinking into my doom of stupidity, over and over again I questioned how this had happened to ME in less than twenty-four hours! Yesterday had been so full of excitement and anticipation; I had opened my heart to the circumstances around me and now I felt like taking a U-turn and going home.

Monday morning offered some clarity of mind. I sat down

with my backpack and pulled everything out and spread it out all over my bunk. Thank God I had stashed the receipts for my traveler's checks in the secret bottom flap!

As I pulled out everything else from flashlight to maps, there sat my empty journal waiting for my exciting story to be written. My bandana fell on my bikini top which caught in the back pouch of my daypack and there it was, my IYH Membership card with a photo! Maybe, with any luck, the US Embassy might consider this proof of identification and reissue a new passport.

Most of that day was spent visiting banks and the US Embassy in Auckland. I felt reluctant to make a collect call to my dad that day to inform him of my losses, but knew he'd appreciate hearing I had arrived safely. Pools of tears welled in my eyes when Dad suggested I return home. No one could truly understand the months of planning I had spent to make this trip a reality. *How could I give up so quickly when I'd come so far?* There was no one who could save me but myself, at this moment.

******

Last year when I had considered the idea of extended travel, I was aware of my good fortune in having a great job with a smart boss. Not only was I getting paid well, but I was absorbing a free law degree as a legal assistant. I know it was crazy to walk away from a decent job that I was feeling confident and fortunate about. But my intuition sensed there was something more, something bigger, waiting for me if only I surrendered to the unknown blank pages of a life as yet, unlived. Here I was at age twenty-seven, still in my innocence and not worried about the future. I had plenty of time for my *laissez faire* attitude. The work-a-day legal loads which backed up to my desk and the drama of liability clauses versus contributory negligence would remain regardless of whether I stayed or left. The legal manipulations of insurance companies versus attorneys would be a lifelong stream of endless paperwork; legal work would always be there for me, so I QUIT!

****

Monday morning the bank offered me a partial cash advance for my traveler's checks, but I needed to wait forty-eight hours for them to verify the loss. The visit to the United States Embassy and reissuance of a stolen passport was a bit more complicated; there would be an investigation, many forms to complete, and numerous telephone calls to folks back home to verify who I was and where I'd been employed. If you can only imagine a time before the internet, slowness was the norm. Thirty days was the minimum wait for a reissuance of a new passport. I was directed to a nearby business for a new passport photo, then delivered the sad portrait back to the embassy. I knew my wallet would probably never be found; addresses and all contact info went with it; all I had to offer the embassy was stored in my memory bank brain. (*how'd we ever get along without cell phones?*) After spending such a long day traversing the government and banking bureaucracy, I wanted OUT of this overwhelming city!

CHAPTER 2

Waiheke Island, January 16

A fellow traveler suggested I take the ferry across the gulf to Waiheke Island. There I would find a private hostel (no curfews) with a short walk to several beaches. As light sprinkles began to fall in Auckland, I boarded the commuter ferry to Waiheke. It was a pleasant seventeen mile trip across Hauraki Gulf as we left clouds looming over the city of my sorrows.

The ferry was full of locals heading home from work and I enjoyed 'ear-wicking' their light-hearted conversations of the day. One of the great advantages of traveling in an English-speaking country is eaves-dropping on those around me.

As we came into view of the island, I noticed very few structures. It appeared that most of the island, covered in idyllic green pastures, was saved for sheep grazing. We neared the dock while many commuters rushed to formation as they scrambled over the railing and jumped onto the dock. I patiently waited for the ramp to be lowered so I could hoist my heavy pack up onto my shoulders.

Within moments, I was met by Terry from the island hostel; he vanned me and another traveler back to his place. The rooms were nothing special – just mattresses on the floor divided by curtains, but everything looked clean. I walked into the kitchen area, where I saw a spacious sundeck and was handed a beer. I felt immediately welcomed.

******

The next morning, I was eager to explore some of the beaches I'd heard so much about, so I headed off to Palm Beach.

Waiheke Island consists of approximately eighty-three miles of rocky, hilly coastline, but saves almost twenty-five miles for pristine beaches made in paradise. Within a ten-minute walk, I found a serene spot on the beach and baptized myself in the warm South Pacific. A feeling of vitality filled my veins!

This is exactly why I am here! I exclaimed to the world.

I strolled back over the hill towards the hostel and saw windsurfing sails darting in the wind in a nearby cove. My feet immediately detoured that direction and once I arrived on Oneroa Beach, I noticed several windsurf boards for rent. Pure delight and joy lured me to rent one!

Secure in my foot straps, I floated over the turquoise-clear waters feeling my confidence returning, filling my spirit just as the wind filled my sail. The afternoon winds blew harder and swifter and, in the excitement of my jubilation and with enough speed, I attempted my first head dip! I leaned over backwards and tipped the top of my head into the water. It may have not been the most graceful maneuver, but I stayed on the board, tacking into the horizon! Maybe it was the warm Pacific waters and not having to wear a wetsuit, but I couldn't stop sailing. My arms screamed with abuse and, in my moments of euphoria, I lost perspective and blew downwind a bit farther than I had intended. I casually walked the sail and board back along the beach to where I had started, all the while yelling out, *I love this place!*

After I returned the board, I sat on the beach just breathing and absorbing my blissful first adventure. It was so refreshing to be in the moment and forget about everything else. I found myself musing about how much my boyfriend back home would have enjoyed this session with me.

******

I had met Ted nine months earlier, after he had just returned from a six-month adventure crossing Australia with his surfing buddy. My girlfriend had introduced us because he was a "hot prospect." Not only was he tall and lanky with a sharp sense of humor, but he had the added features of muscular abs and strong surfer arms.

Did I say he was a bartender in our favorite place in Santa Cruz, the Cooper House Oakroom!? Becoming his girlfriend offered the additional benefits of complimentary pitchers of strawberry margaritas for my friends and me when he was working behind the bar. So, it was rather a funny memory that, shortly after we met, I introduced the surfer to windsurfing. Starting with Moss Landing sessions, Ted later surpassed me in water starts on a smaller board. He sarcastically referred to my old board as the "sidewalk" of windsurfers; but what other windsurfers come with a teak (wood) boom? We shared a three-week surfing safari to Mexico during our courtship, which seemed to cement our relationship as good traveling companions.

As our months together deepened, Ted became my staunch supporter for planning this adventure. I remember him telling me, "If you don't go now, you will regret it forever." He understood the importance of seeing more of the world. When we said goodbye that sad January morning, he "released me" to my inner guidance, whether I came back to him or not.

******

I returned to my laidback accommodations at the Waiheke hostel where friendly-talkative people stayed. I met Dave from Canada, who I found out was assisting Terry (the manager) for the summer season. Steve was an Auckland native visiting the island for a few days. I met Hamlet; not sure which planet he came from, but he appeared with the sharpest, silliest wits I'd ever met. Another friendly Canadian, Bruce, was hanging for a few weeks with his bud, Dave.

So, there you go, surrounded by interesting men, unspoiled beaches and Steinlager beer! *Boyfriend, what boyfriend back home? Remember, I have no proof of who, why or where I'm from.* My personality seemed to soak up the attention while my curiosity about them got the best of me, as the brunt of their jokes. If this was being lost, I wanted to stay forever on Waiheke with these men in merriment and banter. . . and *maybe I didn't really need to go back to collect my identity next week.*

A group of us walked down to the nearby beach to collect clams for a feast that evening. As we stood around the fire pit grilling mollusks till they popped open, I felt nothing less than extreme gratitude for Terry's efforts in creating this temporary family surrounding me. He was an all-inclusive, social guy with a benevolent smile who truly made my visit to Waiheke memorable.

Later that evening, as we were cleaning up the kitchen, several of the guys invited me and others to join them at Rumors Restaurant for a send-off for a local who was relocating to Australia. Local musicians from the island showed up and we danced and cavorted the evening away.

I enjoyed meeting the diverse locals who showed up from the island, from Caucasian to native Maoris. I was honored to be introduced to some of the visiting rugby players who possessed flawless Adonis physiques. My heart pattered and hopefully my drooling didn't show as I conversed with other folks, unable to take my eyes off their firm ebony skin.

As the "single-blond" from California, I had plenty of attention that night – getting shitfaced was not an option after learning my hard lesson in Auckland. Surprisingly though, despite all the delicious men, by and far the best connection I made that evening was to be my new traveling partner, Marsha, an American woman from Oregon.

CHAPTER 3

Back to Auckland, January 24

Marsha had been traveling in and around New Zealand for several months after spending a month in Fiji. She seemed to have made a few useful connections in town, so when she proposed that I stay with her at a friend's place in Auckland, I gratefully accepted.

She introduced me to Hedi, a Persian with an antique shop and home he owned in Devonport. We stayed a couple of nights in his "guest" shed with sleeping pads on a concrete foundation. The rest of Hedi's large home was perched above Devonport Hill with an expansive view of Auckland just across the bay.

Hedi was a member of the Bahai faith, so he introduced me to other Bahais including his housemates Gordon (an American) and his Filipina wife, Sally.

Marsha and I were invited one evening to the exquisite home of Kit and Terri (other Bahais) for a lavish dinner. Their large beautiful home overlooked Rangitato Island, one of the outlying islands outside the Auckland harbor. The dinner conversation that night was stimulating and inspiring as we shared stories of our travel experiences. One of the guests, Faolo, a 19-year young woman, shared her Bahai faith and told stories of the people she met on her recent travels into India and Africa.

The next morning when I awoke from Hedi's back shed, I had been bitten by a spider. My left eye was swollen shut, so I needed to ice my eyelid to reduce the swelling. It was embarrassing to show my face that day, but it was not a day to hide. Auckland's biggest "celebration on the water" was about to begin and I had landed at the right place at the right time – the next stage of England's Whitbread sailing race was leaving Auckland harbor that day!

There were fifteen competing sailboats departing from the harbor and Auckland was Stage Four of a 30k mile, nine-month round the world race (following a route which carried cargo during the 19th century). Out of the fifteen competing boats, there were at least a thousand other boats cheering them on! It was a most impressive sight – probably the largest gathering of boats in the southern hemisphere.

Now I know why people call Auckland, "The City of Sails." There were helicopters with cameras filming the thousand sailboats that hoisted colorful sails and maneuvered around each other. I guesstimated with all the boats and crew members, there were close to seven thousand people on the water that day, saluting the competitors on to the next stage of the race headed towards the South American cape to Uruguay.

It seemed like everyone in Auckland was either on or near the water that day to witness this classic race which had started in 1973 by the British Brewing Company, Whitbread.

Sitting on the expansive lawns of Kit and Terri's property that day overlooking the stream of sails made me feel like

I belonged to a moment so much bigger than myself. Later that evening, Hedi, Tanya, Kit, Marsha and I ordered Chinese takeout, then went down to the waterfront for a Kiwi picnic.

Off to Coromandel Peninsula, February 2

From Auckland, Marsha and I made it as far as the town of Thames that day. It is considered the gateway into the Coromandel Peninsula which is full of adventurous hikes, scenic beaches and waterfall canyons.

The next morning we awoke from our campsite to light drizzles and had to pack up our tent in the wetness. We were both anxious to get going, but we needed to go back into town for some banking business before hitchhiking north into the heart of Coromandel. Shortly after stepping inside the caravan office for check-out of our site, the manager pointed to a young chap in the office who seemed to be heading north, too. I introduced myself then asked "the kid" (he was probably all of twenty years old) if we could catch a ride and pay for his petrol that day. That simple request, inspired by the manager, was the beginning of our wild craze-filled days with David, the "Kiwi Cowboy." He became our chauffeur and guide for the next three days! Right from the get-go, we got along famously, probably because our priorities were the same – exploring secluded beaches and finding quaint pubs.

David was taking a short holiday from his dairy ranching duties. Little did he know that getting away for a few days would include hitching-up with two fun-loving American gals that he'd tell stories about later. We noticed early on that he must have grown up with sisters, because he was so good-natured around us. Considering he was out-numbered by our American-tainted sarcasm, our different backgrounds offered a platform from which we could humorously tease.

By late afternoon, we found ourselves in the tiny town of Whitanga and found a small cabin to rent in a caravan park with a kitchenette and two bunks.

How quaint is Whitanga, one might ask? It has that familiar scent of salt and seafishing and was once an old timber port that harvested the native forests containing a coniferous tree called Kauri, in the late 1800's. Ships sailed in and out, exporting the precious wood to Europe. The town now depends on tourism and fishing, with an annual scallop festival.

When we arrived in Whitanga, the town still had a man-powered ferry which had been in operation since 1895. The crossing consisted of a barge with a strong-armed bloke pulling a heavy rope that connected to the ferry platform on the other side.

Once we made it to the opposite side, we hiked up the ridge into the Shakespeare Cliff area. There we found a historic Maori Pa settlement with a *Wharenui* (ancestral meeting house) trimmed with Maori symbols and heads (Tekoteho) that were all hand-carved and stained brick red. The big meeting house opened up to the circle of smaller family huts which had verandas bordered with even more traditional blood-stained carvings. Sweeping views of the blue Mercury Bay accentuated the location. Some of the carvings used Paua shell pieces for eyes – their reflection felt like history was staring back at me.

It was hard to fathom these Eastern Polynesians traveling by small dugouts in the 1300's to what are now the islands of New Zealand. I was glad David was with us, with his cute British accent, giving us his perspective regarding the island's indigenous tribe. He told me the Maoris named the country of New Zealand "Aotearoa," meaning the 'land of the long white cloud.'

******

We eventually returned to the ferry landing and waited as the operator slowly pulled the wooden barge towards us. It was amazing to witness this time, things being done the way they had been a hundred years or so. On the return crossing, I noticed how the ferryman's muscles bulged with each pull on the heavy rope, stroke-by-stroke, bringing us back into civilization. Definitely one of those "only in New Zealand" experiences.

Once back at the cabin, David offered to teach us gals the art of *pipi* collecting for dinner that night, so down to the beachside we went. Standing in about two to three feet of water, he taught us to dig down into the sand with our hands to find the pipi clams. We gathered quite a bucket full and then grilled them on the caravan grill. That night they tasted scrumptious: mussel-like, slightly raw and salty; slurped down with rice, veggies and beer. Marsha had so thoroughly enjoyed her clam collecting that she had picked more than we could possibly eat. We had at least a dozen left in the bucket.

It became David's mission to "*save the pipis*" which took us back down along the low tide behind our caravan park to return the pipis back into their sand homes.

It was a warm clear evening and the fishermen were still at the docks. Having such a great time with my new friends, I casually pulled out a rolled joint of California cannabis and walked along the low tide, handing it to David. All three of us coughed to hysteria and the rest of the evening became history. At times I felt like I was in an old *Three Stooges* scene as we poked fun and bumped into each other inside our small cabin; we continued late into the night sharing our silly stories from separate bunks.

******

Having a personal chauffeur gave us an opportunity to explore some off-the-beaten-track roads. We exited onto Black Jack Road and followed the steep narrow gravel road which ended at a beach called Otama. Just another picturesque New Zealand stretch of white sands and pure splendor!

We walked down the cliffs, then padded through pristine native dunes towards the beach. Not a soul on the beach to be spotted, and just off the beach, sat the Mercury Bay Islands across the clear cerulean seas. What magnificent and awe-striking beauty! The exclusive island is now privately-owned, hosting celebrities to luxuriate on its five thousand sprawling acres spotted with sheep and private utopian beaches.

My sandals flew off the moment I stepped onto the soft sand, appreciating the gentle surf and native (*Pohutakawa*) trees clinging to the cliffs with their Christmas-red spiked blooms. The sand squeaked beneath my feet as I ambled down into the wetness and reveled in our discovered paradise!

Down the beach we strolled and eventually came to a nearby fresh water creek adorned with ferns that danced in the frisky breeze. We savored our discovered playland for hours as we romped in the waves and then rinsed our crusted skin in the fresh creek rock pools. The quiet of our private paradise was accented only by our laughter and the resident Tui birds with their noisy cackles, clicks and wheezing sounds. It is quite an unusual bird with parrot-like mannerisms and vocalization sounds that I'd never heard before. David recalled they had two voice boxes that enable them to make innumerable sounds. I spotted the most annoying of them in the dunes; he was a beauty with lacy white shafted feathers around his collar. Before heading back to our homey cabin, we stopped at a local small pub to toast our glorious day in the sunshine and wet our whistles.

****

The following morning, we all agreed on some hiking and exploring. We crossed by ferry again and hiked the trail up to Shakespeare Cliff. It was a solid hike with a few steep spots, but well worth the effort. As we made it up over the cliff, to our surprise we discovered a secluded beach down below. From our perch, the cliff peninsula jutted out with views of irresistible beaches (Cooks Beach) below and stunning panoramic vistas overlooking the entire Mercury Bay. The small offshore islands accentuated the clearest visible turquoise waters that I'd ever seen. Some of the vantage points along the trail stopped me in my tracks as I breathed in the stunning views. I made a mental note, "*impressive place to return to, indeed!*" As we continued down a different trail, we found access to another beach called Lonely Bay. Once again, "*heaven on earth*" . . . the sun was warm and the water divine!

With an endless beach of possibilities, I pulled out of my magical backpack two paddles of Smashball (*yes, one of those UNNECESSARY items weighing my pack down*) and started paddling a blue ball up and down when David grabbed the other paddle thinking he could do this better than me. As he caught on to the rhythm, we laughed and frolicked in the sand that sweet day in the mid-morning sunshine. We had a difficult time leaving our secluded beach; I wanted to stay forever, but the day was young and we had tracks to make.

In the town of Tairua we found a small caravan camp for resting our heads that night. Once we had our tents pitched, we rode back into town but found everything closed except for one expensive restaurant and a pub. There is a reason they call us "budget travelers" – we dined on potato chips, peanuts and brew in the pub.

We were up early the next morning for what we thought was a longer ride to our next destination. Opoutere Beach and youth hostel ended up being only a twenty minute drive down the road. We found ourselves taking the short hike from the hostel to the beach for a morning swim and sunbathing. Since David had two more days of his holiday (before returning to his cows in Reporoa), he had decided he wanted to cover more ground and left us gals radiating on the beach. The heartfelt feelings were mutual as we said our goodbyes with solid hugs and thanked David for taking a chance on us for those wonderful few days.

****

Marsha and I appreciated the retreat-like hideaway of Opoutere Youth Hostel. We understood why many locals from Auckland come to visit for weekend getaways. It's surrounded by nature, and happily located in a private spot beside an estuary with no traffic or tourists. The hostel was a converted 1908 school house with white-washed out-buildings and prime views of the Wharekawa harbor. The property bordered a native forest with a few majestic redwood trees. The original teacher's home now holds the community kitchen, a lounge and bunk rooms.

The two of us quickly settled into the old-fashioned hostel and were able to split a private room for a reasonable price. Maybe it was the sweeping views of forest and ocean, or maybe it was the ten-minute walk to the longest stretch of unspoiled beach with a sandy spit for exploring, but at some point, we decided we could easily stay and enjoy the spacious tranquility for at least two more days. Opoutere was the perfect spot to kick back, reflect on our experiences, write, read and explore. We drifted off to sleep each evening with the sound of distant waves as our mantra.

Waihi Town, February 22

I had been on the travel circuit now for over five weeks and was starting to feel a little homesick. Marsha, who had been traveling four months longer than me, could relate to my onset of nostalgia. During dinner at the Rob Roy Hotel, we found ourselves talking about past times back home. We examined a New Zealand map, realizing how diverse and large the various regions were. We had barely covered a small footprint with so many more roads to take. I loved being with another traveler who thought the same way as I did; one who was familiar with the joy and curiosities we both experienced and who also shared a belief in surrendering to the options offered each day.

My memories are bathed with a palette of colors and experiences. Each new day invited us to appreciate the moment to moment unfolding of acquaintances and places. Precious moments offered images of golden waves, honey-colored shells, peanut butter and biscuits; the friendly Kiwis along the way added "the icing on the cake."

Whakatane, February 24

Journal entry: *As I sit here contemplating the ups and downs of the last few days, the rain is falling so heavily that it's creating musical rhythms on the outside downspouts. I wish I were home right now listening to the rain and snuggling with my surfer boy. How I wish he could know how often I think of him. The past thirty-seven days have been difficult with no contact. I've received no letters via "Post Restante" and I am beginning to wonder if he's making future plans without me.*

Marsha and I hitched a ride out of Wahi on Saturday morning with a typical "city" Kiwi guy. I silently said a prayer for protection as he passed vehicles on the curves and tailgated cars, impatiently cursing the "stupid" drivers. We made it to Tauranga in record time.

He kindly dropped us at the ferry terminal so we could cross the harbor to Mt. Maunganui. Once there, we thought we'd find a budget accommodation, but we found tent sites in a caravan park instead. At least the day, which had started out grey and damp, had lightened up and the rain completely lifted by evening.

We both explored the area by foot and discovered "the mount" (as the locals call it) which is actually a huge sandbar peninsula extending from Tauranga Harbor, an unexpectedly large commercial port. One side of the peninsula hosts a sheltered bay of the inner harbor with a few narrow shoreline beaches. On the ocean side there is a long stretch of glorious surf beach, adding to the laid-back surf-town atmosphere.

Mt. Maugnanui prominently stands at the very end of the peninsula and, I was told, is an extinct volcano and sacred Maori site with hiking trails offering splendid coastal views. The volcano cone rose quite dramatically next to our caravan park. We wandered across the peninsula from our campsite and found the local surfers cruising the surf break and enjoying the late afternoon sun.

We walked further down towards town and found the main street was only a block from the ocean. When we stumbled upon a pizzeria and ordered some slices 'to go,' I was reminded of *Pizza my Heart* back home in Santa Cruz. Eating our pizza slices, Marsha and I strolled toward the beach, watching the local windsurfers. The brightly colored sails kept us entertained as they flew across each other's tracks while dodging passing boats and tankers. We rinsed our "pizza fingers" in the shoreline, gazing out towards the horizon and headed back.

Our harborside campsite ended up being the ideal spot for viewing a sunset. It was a good camp except for the caravan atmosphere across the road. I quickly showered and left Marsha napping as I headed down to the water. I enjoyed the slowness of the setting sun and savored my quiet time, reflecting and writing in my journal.

Luck was not with us the next morning; a light drizzle turned up its volume just as we were collapsing the tent. We packed up our now wet gear into our backpacks, then covered them with plastic garbage bags as we headed to the nearest intersection to hitch-hike.

Homesick flashbacks continued as I noticed O'Neil wetsuit stickers and posters plastered on the windows of the town's only surf shop. We stuck out our thumbs and patiently waited for our next ride. Within thirty minutes, we got a lift to the main intersection five km down the road for our next venture to Whakatane (pronounced "Fuc" a tanie). This obscene sounding town was anything but. It was scattered with cutesy suburban homes, a nice athletic field and tennis courts.

Unfortunately, the hostel in Whakatane was almost a mile and half from town; we learned the art of getting lost several times on the back streets.

The last evening, while bored out of our wits, a few of us from the hostel decided to catch a movie in town, so off we went again for the long walk to town. We saw a double feature, a Kiwi sci-fi called *Silent Earth* about the last three remaining people on earth, with an opening flick *Goodbye Porky Pie*, a humorous spiff about a young Kiwi who steals a car in Auckland, picks up a corny hitchhiker, then picks up another unsuspecting hitchhiker and makes it to the South Island with the establishment close behind. It was full of quirky New Zealand humor, which was relatable now that I'd driven with a few of those crazy-eyed drivers.

******

Morning found Marsha and I slowly moving toward the direction of town. We took care of some banking business, enjoyed a quick cafe breakfast and then tramped to Kohi Point Scenic Track. The trail led to spectacular views of the whole region overlooking lagoons, mile-long beaches, as well as a view to the smoldering active volcano, White Island, thirty miles out to sea. I guesstimate we hiked almost ten miles out and back that day. "*Nothing like staying in shape while traveling on the road*," I say. We slept like rocks.

Since the sun never made it out the day before, it made for an enjoyable long hiking day. But the day that appeared before us was raining cats and dogs. Made for a guilt-free day to stay inside and read.

CHAPTER 4

Rotorua, February 27

Sitting here, sorting myself out this morning, in the smelly sulphurous town of Rotoura. This city sits on the southern shores of the expansive Lake Rotorua which is smack-dab in the center of the North Island. Just minutes from this city are hissing geysers, boiling waters, and bubbly mud pools.

Last night, Marsha and I splurged and visited the Tudor Towers (restaurant) for a Maori feed called a *Hangi*, which is a formal cultural buffet with most foods cooked in the ground. I stuffed myself on the world's most succulent lamb, chicken, two types of sweet potatoes, shellfish, refreshing tropical fruit drinks and green salads galore! My favorite salad consisted of greens with marinated fish, raisins & chopped peanuts. A traditional Maori sourdough potato bread was served, along with pineapple and corn flour muffins which required more than one serving.

Construction of the prominent Towers began in 1906 by the New Zealand Department of Tourism as a spa resort for wealthy travelers: a very stately structure, indeed, with half-timbered Tudor architecture, many gables, two towers, and a grand staircase in the entry foyer. As soon as I stepped into the lobby, several ancient sculptures stood out to me and I discovered that the artist, Charles Summers, born in Rome, was friendly with two Catholic popes and was allowed as the only artist with permission to take plastic casts of the sculptures in the Vatican. He sculpted several Greek gods from Carrara marble from Italy in neo classical 13th Century style.

The Towers sit in the geothermal area now known as the Government Gardens. Beautifully manicured green lawns surround the mansion, which are framed by brightly blooming flower beds, lakelets and winding paths. A belt of trees behind the Towers hide the springs and mud pools. The Towers were built facing the scenic Lake Rotorua, encompassing the green, russet and purple hills in the distance. It is unfortunate that the Towers no longer offer therapeutic baths due to the maintenance nightmare caused by the acidic waters and hydrogen sulfide gas which corroded the pipes. Sadly, the baths were closed to the public in 1966.

It was truly an honor to experience the renovated elegant restaurant which included a Maori concert that has been offered for tourists since the closure of the baths. The cultural show was a colorful pageant of numerous traditional *Haka* dances, costumes and music. The women wore stiff grass skirts and danced with swinging *Poi* balls (flax balls at the end of a string) to accentuate their movements. The Maori war dances performed by the men, with their fierce facial expressions and loud thundering voices, made me laugh. They wore their *Ta Moko* (tattoos) proudly as a core component of their Maori traditions and an expression of their tribal affiliations, respect and status.

It is customary for the men to wear Ta Moko on their faces, thighs and arms, whereas the women wear their markings on their chin and lips. I was moved by family heritage stories portrayed through the movement of their hands. The musical voices were soothing and told of a Maori man swimming to Makoia Island to be with the one he loved. Makoia Island is right here on Rotorua Lake, just a stone's throw away. As the sun began setting through the antique stained-glass windows, I noticed a silhouette shadow of a palm frond moving to the music in the outside breeze.

After the show that night, contemporary dance bands from Auckland performed on the sunken dance floor. The Hangi buffet offered with their cultural show, along with the late nightclub, apparently saved the dilapidated building. The night club was renowned as the place to dance the night away for the past three decades; it lived up to its famous legend as we enjoyed dancing and drinking into the wee hours in unusual elegance.

Absorbing the Maori's history and partaking of traditional foods offered us by staff and local performers left me emotionally touched. Someone pointed out to me when I used the word "Hongi" instead of "Hangi," that Hongi meant the traditional pressing of noses, or their Maori kiss, which made me blush a bit for using the wrong word. All of my senses from my tongue and taste to my heart were completely sated that evening. It was gratifying, as a traveler, to witness the local customs alive and well among the families who have kept their Polynesian heritage rooted to their land. At times

I feel like mankind has become too civilized; we keep going forward, faster, and there is no turning back. It was significant to me to observe cultural stories that had not been suppressed by British rule.

******

Yesterday, as Marsha and I were walking down the highway, towards the far end of town, we received a surprising lift from Joseph, a lifetime resident of Rotorua. With our backs to the road and thumbs pointed skyward, he stopped in front of us and asked if we were in a hurry. "Well . . . not really," we responded. "I've got ta make a quick stop on the way, but I could drop ya off next to the highway?" he said.

We jumped in and Joseph immediately pulled a U-turn. He briefly stopped along the way and ran into a nearby Mom and Pop shop. He came out with two small packages and asked, "Don't mind if I drop these to my wife, do ya?"

As he drove, he explained he was on his lunch hour and would we mind having tea with his wife? Five minutes later, Joseph introduced us to his wife as she poured us cups of tea. Little pastry cakes and the cut meat pies were offered as Joseph pulled them out of the bags. He ate quickly, then excused himself while he unloaded his boot (trunk) full of wood.

I sensed the civility of my British ancestors revealed in these two kind people simply sharing tea in exchange for travel stories. I suspected that this was not the first time Joseph had brought home foreigners for lunch, but was honored that it was us that day!

The friendliness of Kiwis, all of it quite genuine and sponttaneous, never ceases to amaze me. Although the years have rushed on since then, I've never forgotten the innocent sweetness of that grey day lunch and have told the story many times since. The experience with Joseph reminded me to "always stay curious and don't let time decide for you."

On Joseph's way back to work at the sawmill, he dropped us at the entrance of two crossroads and, in less than five minutes, our next chauffeur arrived, a South African civil engineer.

CHAPTER 5

Lake Taupo, March 2

How quickly my mood can be altered by dull grey skies. The last five days have run together like pale watercolors. I've spent too many hours sitting inside reading or writing postcards while my energy has fallen into a puddle of homesickness. Perpetual rain robs me of my normal "sunny" personality. Marsha and Diana, a new friend from Canada, had a hard time convincing me to put on my plastic poncho and walk down to the local pub. "Only a ten-minute walk, Pam." Diana coaxed. *"But in the drizzle?"* I whined. After five minutes, their persuasion worked as I reluctantly followed them out the door.

A little funky bar came into view with "Gulliver's Pub" painted on the wooden sign hanging above the door. As we stepped inside the hick town bar, I was expecting to see a jukebox in the corner and two old farts at the bar, but instead was surprised to see the pub hopping with a real live DJ!

Once we found a table and ordered a round, Gil from our hostel joined us at our table. Since most of the local tramping trails were muddy or unpassable from the days of rain, we had all been sitting around for far too long with nothing to do. Diana and I needed to expend some pent-up energy so we got up to dance together on the tiny floor; the next thing we know, we're dancin' with two crazy Kiwis! Abe and Jack introduced themselves as two local farmers from Lake Taupo. I believe those two farmer boys thought they'd struck a jackpot with us, as I don't think it was customary for local girls to dance together. Either that, or obviously these two guys thought we needed dance partners. It was quickly apparent that Abe was attracted to me. Then again, I was young and savored the attention. I couldn't help flirting with him and was fascinated with his brushed blond ruggedness. He had a strong physique with large rough hands. Abe reminded me of Crocodile Dundee (minus a few years) and his accent made him even more appealing to me. Between our party of six, and a few more rounds of brew, the evening got crazier and louder as we danced 'til closing.

I was awakened far too early by the hostel manager, Mark, who woke me by yelling, "Pamela, get up! Hurry, cuz there's a bloke outside on his tractor asking for you."

By the time I jumped up, put a comb through my hair and ran to the front door – there was no one there. Whaddya know, everyone's in the kitchen laughin' at me. *"Funny joke, guys!"* *That blasted Gil, I'll get even with him . . .* I fumed as I walked back to my room. The tables quickly turned, though – because in less than 10 minutes, a phone call came in at the front desk asking for me. It was Abe! I must have told him we were staying at the Rainbow Lodge as he wanted to get together for the day! Touched that I somehow made an impression, I smiled. Since I had already made plans with the gals to take a sailboat tour out on Lake Taupo that day, I asked Abe to meet us at the harbor after 1 p.m.

The morning sunshine was like a spotlight revealing a piece of heaven on the lake. Lake Taupo is the largest freshwater lake in the southern hemisphere and famous for its wild trout. Some eighteen hundred years ago, Mt. Taupo erupted as an explosive cloud of searing pumice ash and gas. Eventually, Beech and Podocarp trees covered the wetlands and surrounding freshwater lake.

We boarded the Ole' Barbary sailboat that morning, an old classic forty-footer which had belonged to the actor Errol Flynn, back in the days when he visited New Zealand during the 1940's. We couldn't have wished for a calmer day as the pure emerald waters mirrored back its shadowed depth. As we motored out to the middle of the deep lake, the captain offered me the steering wheel. *Who me?* What an honor to handle the large wooden helm that Robin Hood, himself, had commandeered decades before.

Our conversant skipper offered interesting and informative bits of info about Lake Taupo. He guided us back into Mine Bay, a private cove only accessible by boat. We maneuvered into this magical world where deep emerald waters reflected ten-meter (30 foot) high Maori images carved into the rock cliff. An astounding creation and lovely gift left by master carver Matahi Whakataka-Brightwell, who, while visiting his mother's homeland in the 1970's, saw the cliffs and decided to use them as his canvas. *Stunning images of a rock carved alligator and Maori faces, the likes of which I'd never seen before!*

Along on the cruise, besides Marsha and myself, was a 17-year old kid named Chris (a fun loving nit-wit); we re-met Ken and Larry (from Mammoth, CA), whom I had met earlier while dancing at the Tudor Towers. What a treat to experience such a clear morning with like-minded curiosity seekers in an intimate setting. As we were heading back, the winds picked up and we helped hoist a sail taking a couple of tacks to arrive back at the harbor. I felt enriched and revived being outside on the lake after three days of rain. *Could things get any better?*

Smiling from the platform was my knight-in-shining-armor waiting for our boat to dock! I thanked the captain for his memorable tour as I stepped off the boat and grabbed Abe's hand. Abe and I then spent a good part of the afternoon getting to know each other better, sitting lakeside eating a bucket of KFC that he had picked up beforehand. I thought, "*Oh, what could be more homey than American food?*" Our rapport was comfortable as we shared our family histories, stories about work and adventures in New Zealand.

Lo and behold, an hour or two later, I spotted Marsha and Ken walking down the shoreline coming our way. They stopped to visit and then Larry followed shortly behind. The afternoon was going by quickly when everyone agreed how dry it was on Sundays with no pubs or liquor stores open. Abe happened to know some friends down the way who ran a hotel and he suggested we all squeeze into his car for the six minute drive north. Our desperately-dry group walked slowly into the hotel lounge where they offered us one quick round of drinks before they had to close. Before we left, Abe slipped into the back and negotiated a 12-pack to go. *Sure helps to know a local on no-alcohol Sunday around these parts.*

Abe drove us back to the lake to another section of beach. As we socialized with our 12-pack, we were entertained by the recreational activities on the water. A water skier zipped back and forth in the foreground, but the real excitement was watching the thrilling barrel rolls of an ultra-light in the pastel sky. Personally, the beach entertained me to no end; it happened to be littered with small pumice stones that amused me into bouts of laughter as I kept throwing them into the lake and watching them float. I'd never experienced floating rocks before! After most of the beer had been consumed, I stepped up the stakes by bringing out my secret stash of California cannabis and rolled a joint as the sun began falling from the sky. Abe's expression of surprise at that moment made me giggle. *"How could this babe be any cooler?"* was the priceless look on his face.

Between my buzz and the others, we all had a memorable time laughing at and poking fun at each other's nationalities. I cherished the moment when I realized most of us had just barely met, yet we acted like long-lost college buddies. The attention I received from the guys was flattering, yet embarrassing when they teased me.

The slow decline of the sun over Lake Taupo filled the radiant horizon with shafts of red, purple and orange gradually getting brighter. The colors intensified as the wispy clouds provided a panoramic sweep magnified by the reflective lake. You just know you're in the right spot at the right time when the Universe delivers a spectacular reminder of its magnificence! And the fact that I was sharing it with my new 'best' friends made the moment that much more extraordinary. The sky and lake continued to slowly melt together and fade into a mix of purple, yellow and orange tie-dye, causing "Ooo's and Ahhh's!" None of us could take our eyes off the stunning display until the sun dipped far below the horizon. The air was especially fresh as I smelled the coolness of the dimming day.

Our gang slowly walked back towards the parking lot, as Abe gently grabbed my hand and stunned me with his dark green eyes – looking at me deeply. I gave him a full body hug and thanked him for hanging out with my "hostel" buddies and told him I would never forget this incredible sunset or the amazing day we had shared. Abe embraced my low back then thanked me with a notable kiss. He made me promise to keep in touch and let him know when I was returning to Auckland.

A day is not wasted if a memory is made.
Unknown author

******

Even with the rain earlier in the week, Lake Taupo revealed its most precious gems day by day. The trails were no longer muddy and after a great night's rest at my now favorite backpackers lodge, I was eager to stretch my legs for an all-day hike. Diana, Marsha, punky Chris, and I headed up to Honey Village, Craters of the Moon, and we even made it to Huka Falls, a thundering waterfall on Waikato River squeezing through a rocky gorge. We found a return trail that led us along the river back to town and covered well over eight miles that day.

I loved the rhythm of traveling now; by surrendering my expectations of what the day might hold, I allowed myself the freedom to experience . . . f l o w. I had been touched by the people that had come into my life and by their offers of kindness. I felt something new emerging in me: *possibly trust of others?* This perspective of faith in others was returning after my initial bad luck in Auckland.

I also found myself questioning my pattern in relationships. Do I use my "protective shield" in relationships with men to hold myself back? To keep from really being free and expansive, have I woven a web of safety around myself and the men in my life? The "US" of my relationships had been, therefore, more important to me than creating my individual self. Was I protecting myself from my own potential in the name of love?

Traveling helps you gain a more accurate and objective view of the world as well as yourself.
Unknown author

✶✶✶✶✶✶

I was a little apprehensive how the day might play out because I was planning to hitchhike to Wellington by myself the next day. Marsha and I had splurged the last few nights at Rainbow Lodge and each had booked a private room. The serenity of my own breathing/snoring was a welcome treat. As much as I had enjoyed my quirky-ship with Marsha, we had spent almost three weeks traveling together. Her company would be missed, but her little annoyances would not.

I felt confident that hitchhiking alone would be an adventure, since I'd seen my share of kindness offered by the curious Kiwis. I was ready to put some miles on my "solo traveling shoes" now.

As I was packing up my stuff, Marsha and I hugged goodbye before she headed west towards the Tasman Sea. Coincidence or not, but following those sweet goodbyes with Marsha, Janell with whom I had spoken several times in the kitchen, came up to me asking when I was leaving for Wellington. Janell had short-streaked blond hair and a chirpy personality that I resonated with. She was originally from Wisconsin, but had been staying with Mark and his wife, the owners of the Rainbow Lodge for the last five weeks. She had taken a reprieve from her travels, staying on at the lodge to help clean in lieu of paying for her room and board. She was getting antsy to continue traveling south when our paths crossed. My new hitching partner had been offered!

Mark drove the two of us to the nearby crossroads and within five minutes an older man stopped who happened to be driving the whole five hours to Wellington, direct! I thought we might be spending the day from outpost to outpost town, hitching with several riders, but... *Whaddya know, the law of attraction timed to perfection once again!* Our first chauffeur, Jack, introduced himself and told us he was driving all the way to Wellington to participate in a lawn bowling tournament for three days.

I felt a bit heartbroken driving away from Lake Taupo because I was leaving behind vivid memories of the wonderful friendships I'd made. The crystal blue waters of the lake reminded me of the genuine conversations I had had with my fellow travelers as well as the locals. The connections I had made felt deep and enduring.

As we were driving away from the lake, I wanted to embrace the familiar silhouette of the mountains and their snowy-topped crevices. I had waited patiently that morning for the clouds to clear (which they had not) so I could snap a photo reminder of the majestic beauty. Just as I was experiencing that missed moment, Jack pulled to the side of the road. *"Do you want to take a photo?"* he asked. *"No hurry, Hon."* I stepped out of the car and breathed in the wide-angled vista. As perfect as it was in my heart, it would never do justice on film. During the long drive that day, I was reminded of little Chris, who was backpacking into those mountains that day; I envied his spirit and knew that he deserved the perfection of that day.

Good ole Jack stopped an hour later and after lunch he bought a watermelon to share with Janell and me; a little later he stopped for ice cream. I knew this was the reason I wanted to visit New Zealand – for the hospitality of a bygone era. They say visiting New Zealand is like experiencing California some forty years earlier. The trust and innocence of these people had not yet been tainted by the influx of US and European travelers yet to come. Time slows down in the Southern hemisphere. There is no better experience than putting yourself out there in the world and letting patience present its gifts. I honestly believe that traveling solo offers so many more opportunities to make new acquaintances than if you were with a partner or tour group. I've noticed that German travelers seem to stick to their clique and rarely socialize outside their circle; how unfortunate for them, while the world presented many more occasions because I was open to the moment. I am always in awe of kindness given so freely, expecting nothing in return.

Wellington, March 3

Our arrival in windy Wellington was right on cue. As we were driving into the city, the rain poured down and the winds began to blow. It had been a spectacular morning when we left Lake Taupo earlier that day; now a drizzly grey set the stage.

Janell and I did a quick walking tour of downtown, dodging raindrops and cold gusts of wind coming off the Cook Strait. Since Wellington was chosen as the Capitol of New Zealand, it had stately government buildings and an industrial port as its main infrastructure. We walked around the parliament buildings, then found an uphill tram from the neighborhood of Lambton Quay that took us up to an overlook of the city and the neighboring botanical gardens. I'm sure Wellington has its charm, but to me, it was just another large industrial port with a commercial harbor. Janell was planning to stay in Wellington for a few more days, but I had seen enough and wanted to move onward.

I was slightly – okay, actually, really bummed – when I arrived at the Wellington IYH hostel and found no letter or note from my boyfriend back home. I'd received letters from Mom and Dad and they deserved a handwritten response, but it felt like there was no other option than to assume Ted had gotten on to other business at that point without me. *I know I'm gone, but I haven't forgotten HIM!* I thought. With or without his correspondence, my adventure was bigger than US. I had so many more unimagined places to visit, so *to heck with him.* I carried on . . .

******

I boarded a deluxe ferry as we pulled out of Wellington harbor the next day mid-morning. The old grey city faded into the clouds. *"Crossing the Cook Strait should be a breeze on this new luxury ferry."* I thought. Not only could the ship carry upwards of 1,000 people, it could transport 200 vehicles. The facilities on the *Arahura* ferry included two spacious passenger lounges, a food court, bar, video arcade, a play area for kids, outdoor observation decks, and a TV lounge.

I spent the first forty-five minutes climbing stairs and exploring all the different decks and cargo holds, then found myself in the lounge bar enjoying a round of drinks with Ian (from London) and a guitar strumming' Kiwi. As soon as we got out into the windy strait, the large ferry felt like a bobbing toyboat in the chop, as we started rolling with the rough seas. I was having problems standing after one drink and feeling a bit queasy, so I excused myself and headed to the front passenger lounge to close my eyes for a bit.

Not knowing what lay ahead, I felt a bit nervous but kept telling myself, *Just be yourself, and be in the moment. Be curious and remain calm.* I probably napped in the rocking ferry for over an hour before I felt the vibration of the engines gear down and noticed the ferry slowing down. The border of wooded land crept closer as we motored into an arm of Queen Charlotte Sound, the largest channel taking us to port. Looking out the windows, I was surprised to see middling hills rising on both sides of the ferry, as our captain maneuvered precisely through the seaway. It was another thirty minutes before we landed at the diminutive Picton Harbor. The adventure continued . . . and I was almost unable to contain my excitement as I stepped onto the South Island.

Chapter 6

South Island, Havelock

There was a bus waiting next to the ferry landing and Ian quickly caught up to me and asked where I was headed. I mentioned the youth hostel in Havelock as he followed me onto the bus. Like a puppy following me home, Ian was tall with long streaked hair, a sexy goatee, but wore the defiant look of a bad child. Thirty minutes later, the bus dropped us across the street from the Havelock Hostel.

Like stepping back in time, our hostel was another converted old schoolhouse, with steep green gables, elongated windows and a wood-aged interior. I found the staff at Havelock very friendly and well informed of their region's highlights. One of the hosts suggested a visit into the nearby sounds, telling me about "the best-kept secret" which was catching the mailboat on Wednesdays (only $14, including lunch) which delivered mail twice per week throughout the sounds.

It so happened that the Wednesday mailboat departed from Havelock the next morning at 9 a.m. Ian and I made sure we were at the dock bright and early. We were told that we would be stopping at four remote residences before heading to St. Omer Resort. I was glad the weather was cooperative as it had been threatening rain when we departed. We slowly motored along miles of overgrown coastline, viewing faraway coves throughout the endless arms of the sounds. I settled into our boat ride as the constant hum and vibration of the motor soothed me into a quiet mood. I started hearing in my head:

"The mate was a mighty sailing man, the skipper brave and sure.

Five passengers set sail that day for a three-hour tour, a three-hour tour.

The weather started getting rough, the tiny ship was tossed.

If not for the courage of the fearless crew, the 'mailboat' would be lost."

. . . with GilliDan, the captain and his skipper, too

a California blond, with a London Lad . . . here on Malborough Sounds.

On a map this region looked small, but I was amazed by the untouched spacious wildness it encompassed. Marlborough Sounds covers some 1,500 miles of peninsulas and islands which lie at the northeasterly tip of the island. The Sounds consist of a huge network of sea-drowned valleys created by downward settling land and rising sea levels. Endless wooded hills and ridges protect fingers of secret bays and, if you turned your head to the right or the left, there was an isolated private cove up each channel. I'd occasionally spot a holiday home on a remote shoreline, or a distant fishing resort with bobbing rowboats anchored near their tiny docks.

For lunch, we stopped at the small resort called St. Omer with a private beach and dock. Mutual laughter began as soon as we exited onto a small wooden floating platform and our skipper, Dan, pulled the long rope to shore without any wobbly-legged guests falling off. Once on land, we were invited inside the charming British home for a sit-down lunch with large picture windows looking out at the demure cove. Our first course was a delicate mussel soup with bread, and then we approached an open buffet of sliced meats, cheese and apple toss, chilled salmon, rice salad and a jiggly Jello dessert. The meal alone was worth the boat fare we'd just paid! For two hours we were welcome to explore the grounds, take a bushwalk, go for a swim, or paddle one of their kayaks. A beachside lounge chair called to me as I digested my meal, happily enjoying the jewel-tone waters gently flushing the sand.

After our small crew boarded the mailboat and were about ready to take off, I remember seeing the skipper roll-his-eyes in dismay. Not sure where she came from, but he noticed one woman at the dock waving papers in her hand. It turned out to be the New Zealand census taker who needed a ride back to Havelock. We watched with bemused humor as the skipper went through the whole ordeal of pulling the floating platform back again to load just one passenger. I was officially counted as a "foreign tourist" that day in their census.

We motored around one land hook, then went slowly past another cove when the skipper pointed us back into a deeper unknown channel. Apparently, we would be visiting a local mussel farm that day as we slowly maneuvered over to a distant buoy and cut the engine. I noticed the floating buoy lines in grid patterns beyond us. The favored green-lipped mussels grew on ropes below the surface that are kept afloat by the large oval buoys. We were told the mussels feed on plankton and microscopic sea creatures filtered out of the water as it flows past. Captain Dan started pulling up a heavy thick rope that had been growing mussels for almost sixteen months. It was extremely heavy and loaded with three to four inch specimens with emerald lips and brownish/green shells. The skipper quickly fired up his portable bar-b-que attached to the stern and placed them on an open grill. The shells cracked open one by one over the heat. I was taken aback for a moment when I saw the flesh colored meat inside the shell as I slurped up an exotic female yoni. They were so delectable and juicy – oh so fresh! Once we broke open the shells, we used the empty halfshell like a knife to pull the meat away from its muscle. We ate a pile of those tasty mussels then washed them down with chilled Steinlagers from the tiny wet bar. Oh my! The sensuous sensation of salty warm mussels in my mouth merging with a perfect lager became a sacred moment in my time/space continuum! I still think that moment may have embodied the most quintessential moment of all my Kiwi experiences!

On the dark quiet waters off Kenepura Sound, our small group toasted our good fortunes sharing this delicacy. I enjoyed meeting Sharon, who was visiting from Palmerston North (N. island), and I was glad Ian had followed me to the boat that morning as he impressed us all with his London rock-star personality. The purity of that day, while tasting the local harvest and sharing it with a handful of guests, on a mailboat no less, would probably not happen in my lifetime again.

The Marlborough Sounds currently generate three-hundred million dollars, including two-hundred and eighty million dollars in exports each year from the sale of frozen half shells, mussel powder and oil that can be used in the nutraceutical industry. Commercialized farms have forever changed the industry and the landscape of those hidden inlets.

I remind myself sometimes . . . *"Isn't it reassuring to know that some of the best days of your life haven't yet happened."* Well, it did that day.

After our all-day cruise, returning to the Havelock dock was like stepping back into the 1940's or 50s. Next to the Glenmore Cruise office was a tiny souvenir shop with a pub on the other side. As we walked back to the old schoolhouse down the one lane road, I noticed Havelock had an English tearoom right next to the main post office building. A little further down on the right was the one and only dairy farm that sustained this small community set outside of time. I was reluctant to leave the area and would have loved to stay and meet more characters, but I felt the need to keep moving down the road. I assumed Ian had been touched by the charm of Havelock, too. He wanted to stay a little bit longer and tried to convince me to rent a house in the sounds for a week. *Alone with him? Egad, No!*

Then again, the famous Abel Tasman hike was calling to me on the other side of Nelson town as soon as I could get a short bus ride, forty-seven miles away. *Decisions, decisions – where to go and what to do?* Think I will leave it up to fate and what the weather Gods offer the next day. I noticed a different sense of place now that I'm on the South Island, where the pace of life moves slower than what I am used to and the temps are a bit chillier, too.

Nelson, New Zealand, March 6

If there is a place I could pick to stay and live in New Zealand, then Nelson would be a great choice! Backed by rugged mountains with distant views of the Tasman Bay, Nelson is known to be the sunniest region on the South Island. Nelson was a nice little city with an air of prosperity that was reminiscent of a Hollywood movie set of the 1950s. It's main street was lined with handsome buildings, a country general store, a bank, a fine bistro or two, a bakery café, and a bookstore with lovely Victorian homes scattered on the out-skirting grid. Nelson has now grown quickly to become a sizeable city with a surrounding population of almost fifty-thousand people!

Nelson has long been a magnet for working artists and is known for its culturally idiosyncratic creators of pottery, glass blowers and weavers, and now wineries have sprung up and are spotted on the surrounding hillsides.

Rural homes, farms and my hostel were located outside the downtown region. I admired the brightly colored Victorian homes in teal, sky blue and yellows one morning on my long walk into town. After cashing a traveler's check, I found a quaint Euro coffee shop and stopped in for a great cup of java. I wandered further down towards the water and saw Port Nelson protected by the boulder bank of rock, a thirteen kilometer bank of rocks offering safe harbor. On the protected side of the rocks was one of the lengthy, golden-sand beaches typical of Nelson.

Nelson is the gateway to the Abel Tasman National Park, a popular three to five-day tramp-about, encompassing tawny-colored beaches, granite cliffs and frequent stream crossings. The trail offers exploration of the luxurious native bush and flora with varieties of birds, seals and dolphins to spot. I was looking forward to the Tasman hike that I'd heard so many wonderful reports about . . . and yet, amazingly, a different sort of opportunity was offered that I could not refuse.

My fellow hostellers offered up a seat in a car heading to Christchurch, some two-hundred and fifty miles south to the east coast. If I'd chip in for petrol, the seat would be mine. It would be my ONE and only opportunity to see Dire Straits in concert the next day, March 7th. Being a music lover, as well as a naturalist, passing up the Abel Tasman trek was a difficult decision that haunts me to this day. It has been permanently parked in my consciousness – forever calling me to return and fulfill my destiny of exploring the Tasman shores.

CHAPTER 7

Christchurch, March 7

Decision made . . . and off I went in a car full of strangers, destined to see the one and only Mark Knopfler! Being a British band, Dire Straits preferred to tour in 'Her Majesty's' countries. Prior to that time, I was not aware of them ever appearing in the United States. I was reminded of one of the greatest lessons of traveling:

> *"You must be willing to let go of your expectations to surrender to the undercurrents of opportunity."*
> Unknown

Four hundred kilometers later, we arrived in Christchurch. The driver dropped me at the Latimer hostel, the place noted on my piece of paper. The rooms were full, the beds all taken, but they were offering floor space. I took what I could get, as it was obvious the city was full of people who were attending that evening's concert.

The hostel host told me if I took Bus #12 to Lancaster Park, the rugby stadium was next to the park. I might find tickets available at the gate, but no one knew for sure. I figured, *"When in doubt, go with the flow."* I was feeling alone and not very confident of what I was doing or where I was going, but I went anyway and found Bus #12 a few blocks away and happily jumped aboard. Mind you, I was operating by the "seat of my pants," as I knew the concert was only hours away and I still had no ticket. With Lady Luck on my side, I found the box office open with remaining tickets. Woo Hoo!

People were arriving and milling around the streets with electric excitement. I strolled a few streets into the neighborhood before I came across a small diner that served homemade Bangers 'n Mash that I washed down with a beer. I took my time, writing in my journal and slowly eating before the concert started.

When I arrived back at the stadium gates, scores of people had already been let in as I walked down the street headed to the end of the line. There were moments I felt entirely out of place and alone – everyone there seemed to be with friends enjoying the party atmosphere. Yet, the greatest advantage to being "single" at a very large event is the ability to squeeze and maneuver through crowds. Once inside, I headed towards the front of the arena and made it within twenty feet of the stage.

Next thing I knew, I was surrounded by three very large Maori men who tapped me on the shoulder. Panic and fear initially screeched through my veins until they smiled and offered a "super charge" hit off a very fat doob. I accepted their "neighborly gesture" and smiled my appreciation. Within seconds, my anxiety vanished. I introduced myself and told them I had come from Nelson that day. Once they realized I was really from California, they acknowledged me like a little sister. I breathed that in – how safe I felt now that I had Maori security at my side. I started laughing at myself for being so silly in thinking I was alone, surrounded by twenty-five thousand people!

As Mark Knopfler hit the stage and started singing, *Money for Nothing*, there was no other place I wanted to be! The sound of Mark's gruff voice while playing his distinctively unique surf guitar (a Resonator guitar), carried me into an exquisitely lovely dreamscape as my body moved in rhythm. Once I opened my eyes, the sexy sax player was belting-out a solo so close to the edge of the stage, I felt I could almost reach out and touch him. My high was intensified by the bright lights and dry-ice effects! To this day, every time I hear the song, *So Far Away*, from the **Brothers in Arms** LP, it takes me back to that moment and reminds me of exactly how I was feeling… *so far away* from my homeland, but blessed by an appreciation for my go-for-it attitude!

Day two – Christchurch

The move to the Avon View Lodge the next day became a step-up after my first night at the Latimer, where I had slept on the floor with a dozen other strangers and their well-used filthy bathrooms. Now, I only had three other beds in my room and everyone seemed to be courteous and friendly. I loved being in a homey room with an antique dresser and mirrors – enough mirrors that I didn't have to share with another guest.

I did all my laundry that day for twenty cents! The air was so warm outside, the breeze so light, my clothes dried on the lines in a couple of hours. I loved how this weekend had unfolded with its own magic. Everything had flowed perfectly and I enjoyed the companionship of my own best friend: me, myself and I. I was elated that I decided to jump at the chance to see Dire Straits – no regrets!

I decided to explore a good deal of Christchurch that next day by renting a bicycle. I headed to New Brighton Beach, not realizing how far it was from town. Since I took the scenic path, of course, it ended up being a ten to eleven mile round trip ride – but I found Christchurch to be the perfect bicycle-friendly town since it's mostly flat.

Christchurch is called "the Garden City" because of North and South Hagley public parks which surround most of the city. It's home to the University of Canterbury, the Deans' house at Riccarton Bush, the Canterbury Museum, the Antique Boatsheds along the Avon River, and my favorite, Cathedral Square in the heart of Christchurch. Christchurch became a city by Royal Charter in 1856, making it officially the oldest established city in New Zealand.

I discovered the Heathcote Estuary that day by following the Avon River which provided early Maori settlements with eel, fish, wood pigeon (*Kereru*) and food plants such as *raupo* or flax for making baskets, clothing and roofing.

To the west, the city is flanked by Hagley Park (approximately 75 acres), the most famous of all the many parks in Christchurch. It has botanical gardens that contain mature trees, giant rhododendrons and native ferns in every size with great names like: Crown Fern, Mountain Tree Fern, Tangle Fern, Spider Fern, and Comb Fern to name a few.

The Avon River, which prominently weaves through town, is reminiscent of old European cities with sturdy British brick homes standing across the river. I lost count of the many stone-constructed arched bridges crossing the winding river at several main intersections. The shallow river meanders slowly through town with beautiful river banks built up with green lawns, weeping willows and flowering trees.

I found the Avon River to be the romantic charm of this town. The slow quiet river absorbs the town's character as it passes gothic stone Revival buildings and Tudor homes decorated with flowery splendor! Pride in their heritage was obvious. What a delightful way to explore and see more of Christchurch, cruising along by bicycle, with my palm cassette playing songs like Steely Dan's "I.G.Y." in my earphones: *"What a beautiful world this will be . . . What a glorious time to be free! We'll be eternally free, yes, and eternally young."*

While taking a walk that Sunday evening after dinner, through one of the many commodious parks, the town felt devoid of traffic and people. Next door to my quarters, outside the window sat the traditional Fire Station No. 4, reminding me of an English storybook scene. Hours later, while trying to drift off to sleep, the noisiest of cars and motorcycles kept passing by. The traffic noise disturbed me, as the fire trucks slumbered next door. Eventually, I drifted off into a pleasant dream.

Day three – Christchurch

The weather was marvelous as I headed down to the Central Post Office in Cathedral Square to check whether I had received any 'general delivery' mail. The classic post office, originally built as the Government Building, is located in the geographical center of Christchurch. It was built in grandiose Italian fashion with red and white painted bricks and a four-sided clock tower that dated back to 1879.

Unfortunately, no mail awaited me. Across the square sits the high-towered Christchurch Cathedral built in 1864 in more Gothic-revival stone. The country's first public bronze statue of the city's founder was unveiled in 1867 atop a pedestal just opposite the cathedral.

I loafed around town most of the day after checking on bus service to Dunedin. I also did some comparison shopping on the large selection of beautiful wool sweaters available in the various local shops. I felt like a sinus cold wanted to get the better of me, so I found a small health food store and bought some bee propolis. *"Bee protected,"* I say.

Shortly after lunch, I headed back down to Cathedral Square to see if the infamous Wizard was lecturing in the Square. Instead, I found a born-again Christian being chewed up and booed by bystanders; then on the other side of the square, a juggler was trying to earn his keep. I was disappointed when 1:10 p.m. rolled around and still, no Wizard. I took off, cruising around the block on my bicycle, returning fifteen minutes later to find the Wizard high on his step-ladder pulpit!

The pontificating professor, who has become something of a national icon, was wearing his long black robe and his wizardly pointy hat. The Wizard has been known to speak at the square during lunchtimes since the mid-1970's: he's an English-born, London-educated comedian, magician, and politician. I was told he had graduated in London with a double degree in psychology and sociology and taught for years in the university system in Australia before formally migrating to New Zealand. The New Zealand Art Gallery Association stated that The Wizard was an authentic living work of art! Then in 1990, the prime minister of New Zealand appointed him the official "Wizard of New Zealand."

The Wizard loudly proclaims his opinions, and his politics, with humor, wit and pervasive argument. Some of his opinions make one stop and think . . . such as, his view of men being wimps because they want their mothers' love and approval. Some of his other topics – like "keeping women in their place to serve men" and "always looking up to their men as God" were ghastly, but probably served to get reactions from the crowd. He's obviously an outspoken 'radical' professor needing a venue to continue his lectures. The banter by the bystanders becomes the direction he follows. I found his opinions comical, sometimes informative, especially while cynically mocking the average family system of "2.5 kids and a house in the suburbs," etc. He spoke with brutal honesty, as he stated, "Americans are the most boring folks. Just look at the rubbish they watch on TV!"

Leaving Christchurch behind filled me with remorse as I realized how intimate and dreamy the Avon River had flowed through me. I'd thoroughly enjoyed my exploration into old-world charm and the accompanying curiosity of identifying new flora and ferns. I even spent some time in the parliament building listening to government hearings; sitting in the high balcony, I was surprised to still see white-wigged men dominating regional democracy. The courtroom smelled of old men and the nattering of their patriarchal posturing.

Eventually, I took myself out to the movie theatre for one last treat. I saw Mikael Baryshnikov in *White Knights,* and I thoroughly enjoyed the perspective of looking at the world through the eyes of a defecting Russian dancer. *What about freedom of choice and expression?* Everyday I'm reminded of the "good life" I have back home. California may be getting crowded, but it's a progressive place where artistic and technical imaginations are born. After the film, I appreciated California even more.

Dunedin, March 12

When I woke up this morning, I was jazzed about getting on the road again. I caught the local bus outside of Christchurch to hitch south to Dunedin. There was already another hitchhiker at the crossroads when I got off the bus. Another guy followed me off the bus with the same idea. With three hitchhikers spaced along the road, guess who got picked up first? The lonely lass, of course! I was dropped off an hour's drive south in Ashburton.

Billowing clouds were forming overhead, so standing outside in the rain was beginning to look like a stupid idea. Luckily, my next lift arrived within just a few minutes – an off-duty truckdriver who took me halfway to Dunedin and dropped me at Studholme Junction before he headed west.

I walked over to a small diner for a quick lunch, then returned to my thumbin' luck at the crossroads. I realized, soon enough, that most of the passing vehicles were heading north, but none were going south. Then the wind started blowing hard and the clouds looked heavy and wet. Fifteen minutes later, two buses arrived at the junction as the drivers stepped out to take lunch at the diner. One bus was marked Christchurch, the other Dunedin. Needless to say, I found a seat on the Dunedin bus, happily convinced that I had saved at least half the fare that day by hitchhiking to Studholme.

Arriving in Dunedin late afternoon, the drizzle had left small puddles on the soaked streets. So glad that I wasn't still waiting on the side of the road anymore! I walked down the road and found the museum and asked directions to the CPO (Central Post Office). My uneventful day turned delightful when I picked up a letter from my best friend, Cheryl, back home! Cheryl sent me great news of home, including a skiing postcard to remind me of what I was missing in the Sierras that Winter. It was so nice to hear from her.

At that moment, walking up the hill towards the youth hostel, I was so glad my pack was twenty pounds lighter after purging stuff in Christchurch. I had boxed up and sent home film canisters, extra clothes, two wool sweaters as gifts, postcards and pamphlets. I surely wouldn't need those things in the tropics in a few weeks.

Dunedin reminded me of Wellington – a very old, damp and salty port town. I am sure I was judging the place by its weather, but Dunedin indeed looked dreary. *Is England really this drab?* I thought. From my room, I had an interesting view of the fogged-in city with a glimpse of the clock tower at the Dunedin Rail Station.

As I was cooking my usual macaroni soup dinner in the communal kitchen that night, I was vibing negative thoughts about how old this gets; traveling from day to day, foreign strangers in each hostel, travelers fartin', snorin' and always making too much noise with their dang rustling plastic bags. I hated my dinner that night. *What am I doing here?* I questioned myself. I just wanted to be home with familiar faces that make me laugh. There is nothing to do in this wet dark city and my encounters reflected my gloom, except for one brief conversation I had with an Asian American from San Francisco.

I went to take a needed hot shower. *What, no line? Nobody? – wow, empty showers!* I took my luxurious time standing in that warm stream of water and then returned to my empty dorm room. Those few moments of privacy were heaven-sent.

I strolled through a few Dunedin wool shops for an hour that morning before the bus took me further south. I was physically aware of dropping into the lower latitude since leaving Christchurch. It was quite chilly as I shopped for another deal on a thick cream-colored wool sweater. Before I considered gifting the sweater to my boyfriend, though, I needed to wear it for warmth. I snuggled into it – wishing it was his arms around me.

******

The scenery that day heading southwest was rather flat and boring – The Canterbury Plains seemed endless. About an hour outside of Dunedin, the hills started rolling – once again they were covered in green and hundreds of puff-ball sheep. Like the saying goes, *"Land of three million people and sixty million sheep."* Or, as I've heard in contrary, *"New Zealand – where the men are men and the sheep, afraid."*

The main highway eventually came out along the coastline for a good stretch. It looked like there could be some incredible beaches down below the cliffs if the sun ever came out. But then again, the best place I could possibly be on such a rainy day was inside this warm bus, watching the miles go by.

I'd been chilled all day long and now felt the tickle of a sore throat. *I can't go backpacking if I'm sick*, I thought with dread. My plan was to tramp Milford Sound for three or four days when I got to Queenstown, but it felt like I might be spending more downtime in town than I had thought. I've noticed how damp weather makes me feel gloomy and down and I was feeling the aloneness of travel the last couple of evenings. Along with that, I hadn't met anyone I felt intrigued to have a conversation with.

Another day . . . another bus ride. At least this bus driver had a personality. Besides being the driver, he's also the parcel delivery guy and the newspaper carrier. Some of the small villages are so spread apart that it is more convenient for the bus drivers, who go through these towns daily, to take care of those matters, too.

The scenery became quite amazing compared to the flatlands the day before. The landscape began to change into more thinned-out brush and trees. As we were coming into Te Anau, the gateway into the Fiordlands, the distant mountain peaks played hide and seek with each twist and turn of the bus route.

Feeling fortunate that I'd had decent weather up until the last three or four days, it seemed Winter was on the horizon on the south island. The temps barely reached 55 degrees that day. I kept saying a silent prayer for, at least, clear weather for my impending tramp over the alps in the coming days.

CHAPTER 8

Te Anau, Milford Sound – March 13

The day before, despite the rain, I could no longer sit around watching the drizzle all day again, so I eagerly caught the 10 a.m. bus to Milford Sound. It was a two hour ride from Te Anau, but the driver kept us entertained with his in-depth knowledge and history of the area and unlimited stories peppered with an array of his cynical Aussie humor. Since I was riding a "tourist" bus, we stopped at a few geological landmarks including The Divide, The Chasm and Mirror Lake. Even in the rain, the views were breathtaking of impressive glaciers nuzzled into the rigid high mountains. Grander than I had ever imagined, these were my first glimpses of glaciers in my lifetime.

I was daunted by the impact of annual avalanche damage with natural erosion claiming a life or two each year as the mountain passes close to the Milford Sound region. Once through the underground tunnel, the valley floor shot straight down towards the fiords. The Fiordland National Park, I am told, is home to fourteen remarkable fiords that have been carved by glaciers throughout the preceding ice ages. Of these fourteen fiords, Milford Sound is considered the most spectacular.

The bus dropped us at the visitor's center at the end of the road and we were greeted by the stunning Mitre Peak – a towering cliff rising over a mile high out of the ocean floor!

I boarded a Milford boat full of tourists and realized that one hasn't seen the totality of New Zealand without a visit to this wondrous place. The prominent Mitre Peak is an over-photographed obsession, but more impressive and subtle were the endless frozen glaciers above us and far beyond our view. I spotted several glacier-gouged crevices spouting elegant ribbon falls with thousand foot drops into the Milford. We passed by the popular Bowen Falls and, since it had been raining, there were hundreds of other falls cascading into the sound as we motored near the vertical walls. We approached a rocky outcropping and saw two Fiordland Crested Penguins. They were unusual black and white penguins with a stern look of authority accentuated by their yellow-white fluffy eyebrows extending over their eyes.

Great Scott! To my serendipitous surprise – on a boat full of tourists, no less – I bumped into Ian from London again! *How many weeks ago had I left him in the Marlborough Sounds?* Getting one of the last few seats on the bus back to Te Anau, I chatted with an Aussie and his Irish girlfriend whom I had met a week or two earlier on the short bus ride to Nelson. Amazing how the circle of familiar faces kept crossing paths.

I was comforted to see a familiar face back at the Te Anau hostel that night. Ian introduced me to two English gals he had met on the Routeburn Track and we all headed down to the local pub for a jug of beer and warm comfort food. It was great to be amongst "friends" again. I appreciated hearing some of the details of their experiences while backpacking through the Routeburn. It was the inspiration I needed. I had been talking myself out of going backpacking – alone. They applauded their experience as the high-point of their travels so far, and deep down, I knew it was something I didn't want to miss.

As we walked back to the hostel that night, I noticed the stars in the clear sky. A good omen, I thought, and just the encouragement needed to start my hike the next morning. The stars were so dazzling in the darkness as I drifted off to sleep that night, I felt aligned with the expansive heavens.

Routeburn Track, Mt. Aspiring National Park – Day 1

I awoke and looked out the window early the next day – cloud cover. *What the heck!* I was determined to go, no matter the weather. After checking some unnecessary belongings at the front desk, I went outside and waved down the 10 a.m. bus to the Routeburn trailhead. As I stepped off the bus, the drizzle stopped! My outlook changed from optimism to enthusiasm. *Make the effort and you'll be rewarded immensely!*

As soon as I started walking the Routeburn, I knew it was going to be a phenomenal adventure. *Incredible scenery around every corner*! As I departed across the southern Alps, I felt myself getting deeper and more intimate with nature. I wanted to be nowhere else but outside, absorbing the vitality of the mountains.

I would be passing through the breathtaking landscapes of Mount Aspiring and Fiordland National Park. There were many attention-grabbing falls that I'd stop for a photo or two and then, after a while, I had to stop taking photos to save film for later (remember 35mm?). There were swinging-bridges over several creeks – first Israeli Creek, then Emily Creek, both luscious with fresh water. After I crossed through a large landslide area, the most wonderful views were revealed of the river down below the snow-capped peaks looking like jewels yet to be discovered. The waters tasted of sweet refreshment and the damp air smelled of rich musky greenery. I hiked up through the beech-forested valley into the heights of the fiordlands with far-off vistas of alpine lakes in the distance. At times, I would stop and listen to the distant sounds. I noticed when I stopped, the clouds and trees moved intensely as my eyes adjusted to my surroundings and my heavy breath and heartbeat slowed. I felt I was on one of the most incredible drugs – a drug called REALISM in the present moment!

Every switchback made me sweat harder and every bit of pain brought me closer, made me stronger, with spirit feeding me hope. Once I'd been out on the trail for several hours, the rhythm of my steps fell in sync with my breathing, creating a deep meditative trance.

Once I arrived at the first sleeping hut, I found several people already staking out sleeping spots. A few more hikers arrived closer to dinnertime. To my astonishment, one of the last hikers to arrive after dinner was Janell, whom I had left in Wellington eleven days earlier! What was the coincidence of

70

aligning back up with her? I gladly moved my sleeping bag over so she could squeeze in next to me and we excitedly caught each other up on our recent adventures.

Reflecting back on the seven miles of 'tramping' I had covered that day, I felt connected by the synchronicity of starting my hike alone, then ending up with Janell by my side. I came to realize exactly why I was there, doing this amazing hike. It was destiny that Janell and I should meet up again to share this unforgettable trek. But I was also aware, whether I was alone or not, that I was taking this hike for many – those who would never see this place in their lifetimes. This is why I'm telling my story!

Routeburn Track – Day 2

Janell and I started out early the next day to get a jump on the other hikers. We were also just so damn excited to be hiking the Routeburn together! The misty morning clouds began to clear as we trekked up and away from the hut, noticing a change in vegetation and scenery immediately. The higher we hiked, the landscape gave way to exposed bare rock and tussock (grass) slopes.

After several miles of switchbacks, and literally, with our tongues hanging out of our mouths, we reached the Harris Saddle summit. Even though we were barely at 5,000 feet, it felt twice that high viewing the Southern Alp peaks across the deep canyons. The Alps were spotted with bleached white glaciers with names like Mount Vancouver, Douglas Peak, Mount Aspiring and Mount Hamilton. The Southern Alps were named by Captain Cook in 1770, who described their "prodigious height." Abel Tasman had previously explored the region, describing the South Island's west coast as "a land uplifted high."

Janell and I stashed our packs behind some rocks and continued our expedition up to summit Conical Peak. I think we climbed another forty-five minutes until we both felt we had reached the top of the world! The view was profound compared to anywhere else I'd ever been and, quite literally, took my breath away! The moment of celebration had arrived: I had been carrying a flask of tequila in my pack for two months (a bon voyage gift from a friend). THIS seemed like the opportune moment to share it! I opened my 'nectar of agave' as Janell and I toasted our good fortunes to meet up and share our summit success! From our 360 degree vantage point, we glimpsed Martins Bay in the Tasman Sea to our west and superb views into the Hollyford Valley and Lake McKerrow beyond. Amazing gratitude is all I felt just sitting on a rock and thinking of all the people who would never see this view (let alone with clear skies). Janell and I had another toast to our un-fathomable visibility overlooking the valleys so far away (Hollyford and Dart River Valleys). If one can imagine the scenery from Tolkien's *Lord of the Rings*, well, there we were, sitting from a vantage point as if looking at Isengard.

We had reached the very top of existence that day! Everything thereafter would be downhill . . . not necessarily good downhill, as we descended a series of steep zig-zags to Lake Mackenzie Hut. Over two hours of pounding steps and loose

Schist stones, my left knee tendon was shooting messages of fatigue. When we finally arrived at the hut, it was completely full of other hikers and we could not see any available space to lay out our pads and bags. With no other options, not having a tent, we continued to the next hut which was over an hour away, arriving after 7 p.m. That hut was full as well, but we were dead-tired and had no other choice but to squeeze in and stay.

Dinner was quick and easy before I rolled out my sleeping bag on an available dining table. As soon as I slipped my legs into my down bag and stretched my back out on the flat surface, every muscle stiffened as I lay there in a puddle of paralysis. The physical challenge I'd put my body through that day was extreme and well beyond its normal limits; it was exhaustion beyond measure. I gave a quick prayer of thanks to my body, my wonderful legs and solid feet which had carried me through thirteen miles of grueling beauty.

Routeburn Track – Day 3

I felt a release mixed with sadness on that final morning when I stepped outside the sleeping hut. Lake Howden hut was located in a beautiful open area surrounded by green grassy fields; the pristine wilderness made me sad for some reason. The tramp out with Janell was wet and miserable, yet very magical at the same time. We hiked three hours in the rain forest past giant ferns as tall as me, mossy rocks, under large palms and then past numerous trickling creeks and falls. I was relieved that the past two days were dry, considering

Milford Sound and the Routeburn are located in the wettest regions in all of New Zealand. I was told the lowlands get up to 300 inches of rain each year! My feet were soaked after ten minutes of walking. I was wearing shorts and my legs were chilled and my damp clammy hands, numb. I resembled a pregnant "war bride," carrying my pack in front under my green rain poncho. Janell wore her army surplus jacket and we looked as if we were walking out of the muddy trenches of Cambodia.

******

Queenstown, March 16

Riding into Queenstown on a shuttle, the only priorities on my mind were a hot shower and a cooked meal. The shower was wet, not satisfyingly warm, but I no longer had mud splattered across my shins and face.

Janell and I found one of the only restaurants open on a slow Sunday night, a Mexican restaurant called Saguaros. We invited Julian (from Perth), whom she and I had met halfway on the Routeburn, to join us for dinner. It was the first "authentic" Mexican meal I'd had since leaving home and I was immediately reminded of my favorite restaurant surrounded by old friends. Just like at home, they immediately served fresh chips and beer! The meal continued with fresh cilantro and limes over the cheesy enchiladas and tacos. It was the taste of comfort on a plate! Soft tortillas, sour cream guacamole & beans made in Mexican heaven. Either that, or . . . I was having a vivid flashback from Mexico due to the last days of depravity, eating dehydrated noodles. The Mexican flavors catapulted my taste buds to another region.

As soon as I heard Neil Young's song, *California Sunsets* playing in the background, I got all solemn and homesick. In my quiet memory, I was transported back to a place called "El Palomar" where margaritas and friends flowed like the Santa Cruz tides. I was obviously missing my familiar comforts and wishing I could share my experiences with some of my old friends back home.

"What the hell! Have another beer, girl; you deserve it! What a hike you've just accomplished! The hike of your life!"

Two beers and I felt . . . GOOD! Then I gallantly walked over to the kitchen and started talking to the staff. "I loved your food so much, guys!" I said, "It reminded me of my favorite hangout back home with all the fresh Cali-Latino ingredients."

I chatted with the friendly cook and an American woman who was the owner of the establishment. The owner and I had immediate rapport and laughed together as I enthusiastically continued to rave about the food. I noticed a few small decorating details of her "California-cool" restaurant. She finally confessed she was a transplant from California, bringing the very first Mexican restaurant to Queenstown, maybe even New Zealand. It was such a time-warp, walking in her door and being immediately transported to my favorite restaurant back home! I wish I could remember the woman's name, because I knew she was bringing a brilliant addition to the tourist circuit. I am positive the chef I met that night, who originally worked there before buying it from the expats, has changed the name of the restaurant to the now very popular, and successful, Sombreros Restaurant.

I awoke to tinkling rain the next morning and immediately noticed the dusting of snow on top of the Remarkable Mountains cradling Queenstown. Janell and I spent most of the morning sharing stories in the warmth of our beds. We caught the 11:30 a.m. shuttle into town for shopping, lunch and toasted Irish coffees for St. Patrick's Day. The "bubbly gals" floated over and took the gondola to the top of Skyline Restaurant for an expansive view overlooking the entire township. The vista alone was worth another St. Paddy's drink at the top of our amazing perspective! There's a reason that mountain range is called "The Remarkables" . . . such impressive high peaks, especially all snow-capped!

The rain slowed to a light mist as we exited the gondola in town. We walked a few minutes before the afternoon winds whipped-up and blew us back to our warm accommodations. Queenstown's beautiful location and its "remarkable" setting will be drawing tourists for years to come. It was obvious to me that it would only be a matter of time before more and more Australians and Americans would be investing in the "après-ski" atmosphere.

Janell was headed with her backpack to Mt. Aspiring National Park the following day, so we enjoyed our last lazy afternoon hanging out together.

The next day, I really wanted to visit Mt. Cook National Park, but there were no tourist buses scheduled on that particular Monday. I reluctantly decided to spend $100 for a rental car; it was beyond my budget, I know, but then again . . . "when in Rome." I asked around the hostel and found two gals from Japan, who spoke broken English, who were willing to split the rental expense and spend a full day with me on the road. *It was meant to be!* I told myself. The drive, itself, was my first experience driving on the "wrong" side of the road, and ended up not being that bad due to little traffic on State Highway 8 through various small towns and stops. It would be a long day of driving over 300 miles, but . . .

Perfect timing seemed to follow me – as another phenomenal day of clear skies greeted us after two days of wet and wind. As I drove north, the magnificent Tasman Glacier poured down the expanse of Mt. Cook – the highest majestic mountain in all Kiwi-kingdomhood! 12,200 feet of towering beauty – her sensual ice flowing forth to reveal her fullness.

This country has some of the most awe-inspiring splendor the world has to offer! I know I keep saying that, but it's true; from the lowlands kissing the seas in the southwest, to crossing the expansive Canterbury plains, the lowlands rise into peaks that grow into massive glaciers. I still can't believe I experienced the living, breathing ice age . . . a witness to thousands of years of geological marvel!

Backpacking up the Southern Alps on the Routeburn Track had given me a wide-angle view of the amazing "Lord of the

Rings" vastness. Appreciation filled my soul for my amazing luck blessed with high-visibility days.

"I am so absorbed in the wonder of the earth and the life upon it, that I cannot think of heaven and angels. I have enough for this life."

Pearl Buck

I drove our rental car up Hooker Valley towards the park and was greeted with bright glacial turquoise waters of the lake resting at the base of Mt. Cook. *Stunning, absolutely stunning scenery as if from another world!*

As we approached Mt. Cook, there were high clouds streaming over the pointy summit in gusts, which then evaporated beyond its pierce with the peak. I later found out that I had witnessed the "Nor'west arch" wherein, "moist air is pushed up over the mountains forming an arch of cloud in an otherwise blue sky."

The park contains more than 140 peaks which stand over two thousand meters (6,600 ft) and over 65 named glaciers. The massiveness of the southern alps is available to any mountain climber, extreme skier or hiker and only asks to be conquered by any number of visitors who keep it busy season-round. I enjoyed spending time in the car with my new friends from Japan that day as we shared our cultures and timid laughter.

Satisfied with my adventures and experiences near Queenstown, I caught a warm bus ride back to Christchurch on Tuesday. I recall it being a very long day and by the time I arrived in town, it was almost dark and rainy again. At least I was familiar with the town and returned to the Avon Lodge, as I comfortably settled inside the study and caught up on my letter and journal writing.

It's in those moments of reflection that memories float back to remind me of who I was becoming and where I was headed. It seemed that the ease of throwing my pack over my shoulder and catching a bus to the airport came from familiarity at that point; eight weeks of cars, buses and boats established my solid rhythm of traveling. After the first three weeks of traveling, there is a cadence that sets in allowing one to forget about time and schedules. I surrendered to the unknown path laid out before me each day and trusted my own intuition. Never had I felt so free from my self-imposed insecurities and expectations.

Chapter 9

Good Endings – March 20

Even though I was feeling sad about leaving New Zealand, there was an anticipated excitement building as well . . .

The most delightful Kiwi I had met, Abe, was picking me up at the Auckland airport! *Oh yeah, how's that for service?* Did I say, *"He's charming"* too?

I caught a forty-seat plane out of Christchurch. Upon landing in Rotorua for a quick layover, I stepped outside the plane for some fresh air and was immediately reminded of where I was – that familiar sulfur smell permeated the air.

Back in the air, for a short takeoff and landing, I floated into the Auckland International Terminal. I was surprised by my lack of anxiety, which I'd experienced months earlier walking down the same terminal. I now walked through the gate as a confident, curious adventurer and the manifestation of my new self was refreshing! This time, I didn't feel like a foreigner in a strange land. This time, I'd have a familiar face to greet me . . .

I had been keeping in touch with Abe by phone during the past few weeks and he insisted that he meet me in Auckland when I returned to the North Island. I would have only two more days in Auckland before I continued my traipsing into the South Seas.

Since my plane had fallen a bit behind schedule, I was worried that Abe would have had to wait for me. Instead, he had been panicked because he had an accident on his drive up from his home outside of Lake Taupo. A rock had hit his windscreen and had cracked it so badly, he couldn't see out of it. Abe had had to stop and break the remaining glass and remove it entirely before he could continue. He had spent the last hour of his drive on the motorway with no windscreen! But Abe seemed to take things in stride and apologized for his delay. I could tell he was embarrassed that he had to drive me into Auckland City with the wind in my face, but I laughed it off because, #1, it was NOT raining and #2, I was back in those lovely north island warm temps! I smiled and picked a bug out of my tooth, feeling thrilled that Abe wanted to see me again and wanted to share some of his personal New Zealand with me.

He drove me slowly to the lovely suburb of Parnell Village. Located in a south-western tenant of Auckland, it was a sunny village rising up the hill overlooking the Auckland outer bay. There were rows of "Ye Olde Worlde Shops" lining the few blocks of Parnell Road, with cute little cafes and umbrellas dotting its charm.

Parnell hosts several beautiful parks, including the main park known as the Rose Gardens. I was captivated by the quaint charisma of the place. Abe explained that, through the years, when old buildings underwent demolition in the whole Auckland region, Parnell Village had incorporated period materials from those demolitions and had "tarted-up" many of the Victorian style homes and turned them into fine dining establishments and shops.

Abe had made reservations with his old friends for an available upstairs studio. When he invited me up to take a look, I was amazed by the wide-picture windows overlooking Rangitoto Island across the bay. *What a classy guy!* The luxury flat had a kitchenette and he had arranged a dozen chilled Steiney's waiting for us in the fridge! I couldn't believe the drop-dead view as the headboard to the room. I was so excited in the moment that I showed my joy by planting a big kiss on his adorable lips!

Abe escorted me down the walkway to a friend's restaurant nearby. He introduced me to Lizzy, the owner. I immediately loved Lizzy's open friendliness as she asked about my trip and the favorite places I'd seen. She graciously served us a superb fresh fish salad on greens with a wink and smile. When she returned, she came bearing plates of flaky corned ham with seasoned vegetables and left us to eat in romantic elegance in the corner. I wish I could remember all the details of that significant dinner as Abe and I shared a bottle of local wine and laughed easily about our histories. The woman I am today blossomed that evening as my shyness dissolved into the dark corners of that restaurant. My voice was strong and enthusiastic as I freely shared who I was and where I'd come from. There were no moments of awkwardness between us as my assertive curiosity bombarded Abe with questions about his family and his move to Lake Taupo. We encouraged each other's character as our passions for life and the common thread between us were revealed.

As we neared the end of our bottle of wine, Lizzy returned and took a seat next to us with a sigh of relief; the main dinner crowd had thinned out and she could finally sit for a moment. She was so happy to see Abe (a long-time friend when he had lived in Auckland) and filled him in on their mutual friends. Lizzy waved to the waiter for a bottle of wine and gestured her friend, Sally, over to our table with her boyfriend right behind. We shared our nationalities and heritage a bit, before the second bottle was brought over by Lizzy's boyfriend, Bill, who came from behind the kitchen. I think we were working on our third bottle of wine when Lizzy brought out her guitar and started singing with a surprisingly angelic voice!

The evening morphed into the most unexpected meeting of friends, all with fascinating tales. I loved the honest blunt humor and ease with which we told our stories – at times niggling each other's versions. Of course, three bottles of wine contributed to our lost inhibitions and non-stop laughter. In the magic of those hours together, we became each other's long lost friends. Before the evening ended though, we were found singing along with Lizzy to Simon & Garfunkel and some 1960's folk songs, including our various national anthems.

Could I have ever been thrown into such a delightful group had I not been traveling solo? Traveling alone can sometimes be scary, but it unquestionably opens more possibilities. It has led me to meet some extraordinary people that I'd never have met if I were with a partner or a girlfriend.

Even though I was seven thousand miles away from my home, I was reminded that "home is where the heart is." As I laughed with Bill, Lizzy, Abe, Sally and her boyfriend, on this, my very last night in New Zealand, I was surrounded by the most authentic people a person could ever find! The night seemed like a synchronized meeting of our wild and radical minds and I was so glad to be part of the mix.

I've always loved the saying, *"Isn't it nice to know that some of the best days of your life are yet to happen?"* And that night certainly stands out as one of them!

I felt so truly accepted that evening as I hugged each of my new friends goodbye and Abe and I departed up the street.

How could I be leaving this amazing country with the most beautiful people I'd ever met?

Abe had "brought me home" by sharing who and what he loves in life. I felt deeply honored that he was comfortable introducing me to his friends. I was intrigued and curious as the thought arose in me . . . *This relationship could become serious if I stayed . . .*

And stayed I did, all night long! Our mutual desires exploded all over the spacious room as soon as the door closed behind us. Some of my sexual fantasies took a backseat to the reality of what that weathered cowboy did to me . . . with his tan, stocky, sexy build and pure Dundee . . . vigor! I'm not sure if we both had been abstaining from sex for a little too long, but I felt like the doors were blown wide open! Our lovemaking lasted into the wee hours of dawn and was equal to an entire circular relationship being condensed into one evening of unbridled hunger!

The next morning, I wasn't sure if my head was spinning from an excess of lovemaking or alcohol. An abundance of love, all at once is like a powerful wave that can knock you right off your feet! The pounding in my head intensified as the blasting sunshine came through those lovely picture windows.

Sweet, sweet Abe had left me some coffee and scooted out early to go drop off his car for a new windscreen replacement. As I lay there with a large sideways grin, I had to congratulate myself, for once again . . . manifesting the most marvelous experiences life can give!

Then reminded myself . . . *See what a good attitude will get you, Pam, if you trust your intuition, push your comfort level and add a touch of flexibility. Wha La . . . You become magnetic to just the right people!*

I slowly peeled myself out of bed for some water and aspirin – hit the shower, then giddily jumped up and down on the bed before settling down with the paper and coffee. I felt like a "pea in the pod" in that large impressive room. I had been deprived of luxury accommodations for far too long.

When Abe returned, we walked down the hill for 'brekky' brunch. We said hello to Bill as we passed Lizzy's restaurant and stopped into a nearby boutique, owned by another friend.

Abe was working his local magic on me, wanting me to stay just a little bit longer. As we sat under a café umbrella on that picture-perfect day, I savored each deep glance into his green eyes as I slowly ate my pastry and eggs; he was more than a handsome bloke; he was a great guy and "great" guys are hard to come by. We laughed at the plump finches begging for our bread crumbs as we finished our meal in melancholy smiles.

I am not sure I understood at that moment that I would probably never see Abe again. That morning, now a flash in time, has left a permanent mark on my heart. It was more than a simple fling or a brief romance. I cherished my time with Abe because he introduced me to Myself. He allowed me to fall in love with my life and who I was. He helped me to break through my limitations and freed something deep inside me. He didn't know it, but he was my savior.

******

I returned to the U.S. Consulate's office to pick up my newly issued passport with a new photo and a new bolder version of myself. *Here I am, World! A vibrant young woman who is willing to live life on her own terms!*

As I walked out those heavy government doors, I felt a transition taking place deep in my DNA, like the emergence from the restricted cocoon of my teens and early twenties. My shy, reserved identity had been slowly shed over these past months. With a new passport in hand, the load on my shoulders transformed into wings!

As I look back on those last days in Auckland, it truly *was* a turning point for my life. I *could* have stayed and created an unknown life with a Kiwi who was grounded, loved by his friends and a believer in fate and adventures. Or . . . I could continue with the unknown journey that lay ahead of me. The beautiful maturing butterfly lifted off those granite steps that day, floating higher and farther towards her destiny!

My encounters with the locals and visiting the striking landscapes of New Zealand far exceeded anything I could have actually imagined! I was initially curious to visit New Zealand's unspoiled beaches and landscapes. But the true surprise was more than its fiordlands. It was the *people* who went out of their way for me! Everyone, from the helpful hostel workers, the local dairy store clerks, the sailboat captain, the pub tenders, the Maori concert goers, and even the bus drivers, treated me with genuine graciousness. Solo traveling inspired me to be more authentic, but also served as a constant reminder of the kindness of strangers and . . . "that you're never truly alone."

It was difficult sitting on that plane for takeoff, saying my silent goodbyes to so much and so many. There was joy in my soft tears as I realized I was leaving, not only a lovely country, but an experience of a place set back in time.

> *Listen to the wind, it talks.*
> *Listen to the silence, it speaks.*
> *Listen to your heart, it knows.*
>
> Native Indian Proverb

Whitbread Race, Auckland Harbor

Routeburn Track

Conical Peak with Janell

Ole Barbary (Errol Flynn's boat) on Lake Taupo

Waka root from Market. Phil, Lori, Pam, Dan & Mike

Kava Ceremony

Bertie with Pam, Lori & Mary

Draniv-i-Ra Village Chief with family

PART TWO

Chapter 10

Viti Levu, FIJI - March 23, 1986

After my four-hour flight from New Zealand, I stepped out onto the island of Viti Levu, as the sultry tropical air slapped me across the face! The air was thick with humidity and had me wondering how I would survive the next month in such a sweaty place! My weighted packs, worn front and back, seemed so much more of a burden in the heavy heat.

I hopped into a waiting taxi headed directly into the urban agglomeration of Nadi. Population: 30,000 in 1980's and 90's, located on the western side of the main island of Viti Levu. The capitol of Fiji is Suva situated on the southeastern side of the island with a population triple that of Nadi. Thanks to my Lonely Planet bible, the taxi dropped me off at my first choice sleeping house or as they call them in Fiji, a *bure* (bur-ay). Sunseekers Lodge sat outside the bustle and grit of main street downtown; location being the best feature, only 300 meters from the junction of Queens Road and the road leading to the high-end hotels.

Airplane altitudes have a tendency of clogging my head. I can be lightheaded for hours or a day after a flight, but this time it was compounded with the sentience that I was still "floating in hormone-love" with my "left behind, but not forgotten"

Kiwi cowboy. Abe's genuine kindness continued to swirl in my head. He treated me like English royalty for those few days of camaraderie and cuddling. After my short-lived days of indulgence, I needed a room to myself – *because I'm worth it!*

Sunseekers Lodge fit the bill with a private simple room with an overhead fan. The petite Fijian girl at the front desk introduced herself as "Mita." She casually mentioned, in slow English, that they offered simple meals from their small kitchen. Their menu consisted of coffee, tea, toast & eggs, basic sandwiches, and the "best bar-b-que chicken" in town.

******

Viti Levu (pronounced Vee-tee Lay-vu) is the largest island in the Fijian archipelago, comparable to the Big Island of Hawaii. It is believed that the Polynesians were probably the first people to inhabit the heavenly islands; later, in 500 B.C., Melanesian people arrived, and the fusion of the Melanesian and the Polynesian peoples gave birth to the Fijian race.

I was surprised to find that most of the inhabitants in the populated city were of Indian descent, known as Indo-Fijians, whose ancestors (approx. 50,000) came as indentured workers from India between 1879 and 1916, and never left the islands. Since then, the biggest threat to the native Fijian population (www.hellenicaworld.com/Fiji/Literature/NormanECabel/en/ARacialStudy.html) stems not from disease but from Indian over-population. While Christianity may have historically been the dominant faith, there are increasing populations of Hindu and Islam practitioners. The city region is over-bred, in my opinion, but I was not planning on spending a great deal of time in the city of Nadi. Island hopping was MY goal! My head was floating in turquoise seas with the anticipation of what was to come.

I expected I might have some difficulty with the language in Fiji, but the service industry had adjusted to the tourist trade by learning survival English. I was surprised to find out that most Indo-Fijians spoke two or three languages, including Bau (standard Fijian) with other villagers, Hindustani with their family, and English with the tourists. The settling Indians of Fiji long ago came from diverse groups, including Hindus, Sikhs, and Muslims.

Getting hit by the wall of humidity and humanity, I was not what you would call energetic, so exploring would have to wait. I was feeling overwhelmed and a bit concerned that I might be coming down with a nasty cold, so I decided to stay on the premises at Sunseekers. I took myself down to the rather modest dining room and bar and plopped down at a small table, in between two fans, and ordered my chicken dinner (probably as organic as it comes – fresh from the back door) and a cold soda from the bar.

A short time after I had finished my dinner and was chasing my drink with a good book, three American chaps appeared at the demure four-stooled bar. Phil and Mike seemed like good-humored best buddies and introduced themselves and their new friend, Dan. All three guys were roughly my age – Dan maybe a few years younger. They were all darkly tanned from weeks basking in the tropics. Phil sported a bushy dark mustache with thinning hair on a dark-tanned head. Mike had curly uncut brown hair and modeled a round beer-belly hidden underneath his khaki vest and t-shirt. And Dan was a blond, blue-eyed surfer, with abs like a washboard wearing a muscle-tank. After visiting and talking 'bout our travels' for a while, I learned that both Mike and Phil were skiers from Mt. Rose and lived in Reno; we were "technically" neighbors and became fast friends. I find it curious that when you find the common thread in your backgrounds, the world becomes a smaller and friendlier place.

The boys convinced me, and two other ladies staying at Sunseekers, into walking into town for drinks and dancing. Little did I know how bad downtown Nadi really was! I was so glad we had some guys to escort us through town. The downtown was over-run with dark-skinned pesky Indians – harassing us every step of the way from their sidewalk storefronts. Non-stop bantering, fake English flattery, and being chased down the street really turned me off. I felt like a walking dollar sign at that point and it left me with a very low opinion.

Mike picked a dive-bar he had heard about as we all walked in together. The Jamaican-beat band was doing their best rendition of a Rolling Stone tune while seated on stools. After a round of Fiji Bitter beers, I'd forgotten about my headcold and the music, as it always does, inspired me to get up and move to the groove, as others joyfully joined me on the floor. The later the evening progressed, the weirder the vibe from the locals felt. Thank goodness Mike and Phil were still there, because I couldn't get some Indian jerk to leave me alone, so they walked us safely back to Sunseekers.

The next day by mid-morning, Phil and Mike showed up at Sunseekers with their bags to check into a simple airy room and get the hell out of their dirty bure. Nadi is quite the slimy city and it's best to shop around for an appropriate place to stay.

I was still having difficulty adjusting to the heat and humidity and couldn't clear my sinuses. I blamed the drastic shift in temperature; either that, or I'd picked up a bug back in New Zealand. No matter what it was, I appeared to be in the throes of a full-blown sinus cold. What hadn't helped my condition either was that, while in New Zealand, I had partaken in the decadent joys of some of the finest dairy the world over; from white cheddar cheeses, home-made yogurts, and milk with thick cream on top. My poor sinuses were backing up on a whole new level. I questioned my need to book a scuba dive trip to one of the outer islands that day, deciding to rest one more day and stay right where I was.

That evening, I joined Phil and Mike for another "best" bar-b-que chicken dinner and had the fortune to meet Lori, from Hawaii, and Mary, from Jersey. They were traveling independently, but were on a similar travel circuit. We curiously talked that evening about visiting one of the Fijian villages, but never took it seriously until the next morning. Mike kept persisting he had a guy who would take us to a Fijian village, but we would need to buy some Waka Root to present to the chief. Waka Root and/or Kava are both from the root of the Kava plant, but the Waka comes from the lower part of the plant which is more potent than Kava. It is Fiji's national narcotic beverage and Mike had been told that you could get the root at the local market. He became so enthusiastic about obtaining some "root" that we unconsciously elected him most jovial group leader. The waka became the joke and banter between us, talking about obtaining our 'contraband': *"Hey man! We gotta get us some root, bro."* I laugh now, because I recently read that Kava is being highly exported to the U.S. and European countries.

All six of us piled into a taxi and went for an exploration to the local market in search of the "waka." At the market I saw strange-looking produce, numerous rusty-colored spices, stacked sugar-cane poles, colorful fabrics and hanging t-shirts. Mike and Phil asked around and then we followed a Fijian to a stall where they made their "narcotic deal." We returned to our hotel with our wrapped contraband, waiting for Mike's driver to take us to a local Fijian village. Although we waited until almost noon, Mike's guy never showed up. Mike was determined to visit a village that day, so he took the initiative and went and talked to Mita in the kitchen. She had previously shared with him that she was from a koro (village) along the north coast. She gave Mike the name of her village. We were told that Draniv-i-Ra village was approximately a two-hour bus ride away. Since we didn't know if we would be back that night, we left most of our possessions at Sunseekers in a storage locker. I brought my day pack with ID, money and a sarong, and then our troupe of Yanks boarded a local bus for Raki-Raki.

Draniv-i-Ra Village

I've always enjoyed seeing new scenery from a moving bus and this ride did not disappoint as we passed expansive views of sugar plantations and pastoral landscapes scattered with thatched huts. We covered a lot of ground in two hours and when our express bus flew past the village stop, two of us confirmed what they had seen, in fact, was a sign for Draniv-i-Ra's roadside stop. We got off the bus at the next stop, then had to backtrack on the next westbound bus where we were dropped off next to a wooden hut with a propped plywood shade – Dranivi-i-Ra's bus stop & roadside mini(mal) mart.

We started walking into the village by a well-worn foot trail and asked for directions to the chief as we passed a young man. The curiosity as to why six Yanks were asking for the chief caused a bit of commotion. It seemed like a few more young men joined us as we were guided to the center of the village. As we neared a circle of thatched huts, a middle-aged man came down the steps from a stilted wooden home to join us. There were linguistic difficulties in explaining our visit, but they all understood the bag of waka root as a traditional offering.

I noticed that our English fell on deaf ears, but our slow physical gestures were understood completely. Customs needed to be followed and we understood that we needed to wait while the village teacher was located so he could interpret for us. We waited in the circle of thatched huts for an awkward fifteen minutes as we watched the islanders continue with their chores or speak among themselves while curiously staring at us. Before long, a tall thin man came down one of the path-ways with several young boys running alongside him. Bertie introduced himself in English and we were relieved to stand on common ground. Bertie was an accommodating Fijian who didn't appear to be "flustered" by the sudden appearance of our troupe, probably due to his familiarity with a classroom full of kids. We shared that we had met Mita in Nadi, who had told us about her home village. Bertie immediately greeted us with open arms, asking of the names we call ourselves. He then went over to one of the stilted homes asking if the chief was available to accept our friendly offering.

Fijian indigenous society is very communal, with great impor-tance attached to the family unit, the village, and their land. A hierarchy of chiefs preside over each village and we were told that the elder chief we would meet was Bertie's grandfather! Then an old man slowly stepped outside his home and sat on one of the top steps; two older women flanked the doorway. Bertie introduced us each by name as Mike stepped up and presented the waka root directly to him. At that moment, I was so proud Mike had done his homework, because it seemed to be the golden ticket – the barrier was lowered and our offering was accepted and we were invited and welcomed into their *koro* (village).

After acceptance of the root, they walked us through their village to another formal wooden building on stilts. Each village has a communal meeting house and a spirit house. The spirit homes are elevated and usually housed the chief. All the other villagers live in thatched grass huts scattered around. As we climbed the stairs and entered, we were introduced and bowed to several elder men who were sitting cross-legged on the floor. This was the men's "watering hole," so-to-speak, and we were invited into their ceremonial drinking spot. Even though this was the men's customary tradition, and local women were not invited, they motioned for us three women to sit in the circle and join them on the floor. Bertie explained how the drink was made by grinding the waka root into a fine powder then mixing it with water in a large bowl. A cloth then pressed and sieved the mixture before it was squeezed into a carved out single slab wooden bowl, known as a *tanoa*.

Our interpreter, Bertie, then showed us step-by-step the custom and protocol of how to drink kava, always starting with the ranking village elder. In a ceremonial setting, every movement involving the mixing of the drink is significant. The straining and serving are all part of a ritual, performed with a high degree of skill and grace and every detail is watched by critical eyes. The pace of the ceremony is governed by measured hand-claps (*cobo*). In our case, a coconut shell cup (*bilo*) was dipped into the tanoa and offered each guest, who must first clap once before accepting the bilo with both hands and then drink the entire contents.

That gulp is followed by all members of the circle clapping in unison three times. By drinking from the community cup, communal bonds are formed, playing an important part in public, business and social life. Etiquette is detailed depending on the function, as it shows respect between two communal tribes, strengthens family ties and reinforces the community's social fabric.

The grog, as it is sometimes called, was slightly filtered and tasted of mud (a recogntion from childhood?). Initially, I noticed a numbing sensation on my lips, then my tongue, and in small doses the drink causes muscle relaxation and feelings of wellbeing. While enjoying the calming effects of the drink, one eventually becomes accustomed to the muddy taste.

It seemed to me we each had two or three rounds. I lost track, but I recall being very relaxed and comfortable in my skin. Enjoying the natural flow of our interactions, with a lot of hand signals, by the end of the third round, there was plenty of laughter as all barriers came down. I felt honored to be participating in this ancient ritual of friendship. I am not sure I understood the significance of the moment, but have since realized how the experience has stayed with me forever.

Our honorary "initiation" into the tribe was followed by Bertie and a few of the men escorting us over to a large open grassy area where a group of very muscular Fijian rugby players were lined up. I think Lori and I blushed when we looked at each other and thought the same thing. I mean . . . *Let's be honest – when do you ever get an opportunity to inspect a team of hard-bodied young men dressed only in a skirt (sarong)?* I'll speak for myself when I say I had a hard time taking my eyes off their strong hairless chests, or the dark curve of a bicep. They had beefy necks, large hands and wide bare feet. Their bodies radiated peak physical strength. We all nodded politely as they introduced us as "the Americans."

We were told that the Fijian team had just returned from New Zealand where they had competed in a major tournament. Draniv-i-Ra villagers were honoring their return and celebrating their victory! *No kidding, and we just happened to walk into the village that day for a victory celebration? Wow!*

The festivities were just getting started as villagers gathered round and we watched the initial procession. It started with a few of the middle-aged men carrying a very large, pink-skinned and gutted cow; it was tied by its feet hanging from a long pole weighted on the men's shoulders. The cow was then placed at the feet of the rugby team as a gift. A few words were exchanged in Fijian as the village acknowledged the team.

I was curious as to what would happen next and watched as they moved the cow to a prepared in-ground fire pit called a *lovo*. A lovo is a large wood pile built with rocks piled on top. The fire is then lit from within the center. After a short while, flames arise and stones fall into the embers as the wood burns away. Once the rocks lose their color and appear "white hot," the cooking begins. Pitchforks and shovels are used to remove the remaining firewood and to spread the stones evenly at the bottom of the pit. Once the firewood is cleaned out, the cow was placed upon the rocks quickly and then covered up in order to retain the heat.

The celebration continued as drumming and chanting began to emerge from the surrounding villagers. I was quite taken and surprised by the jubilation and excitement. Elderly women paraded in next, bumping their hips to the beat of the drums.

Besides their celebratory dance, the women wore wrapped Fijian barkcloth, called *Tapa*, around their bodies. The bark-cloth, made from the bark of a mulberry tree, looked like a heavy stiff fabric which was decorated with traditional Fijian motifs. Each island group has its own characteristic colors and patterns, which range from plant-like paintings to geometric designs. The Tapa is usually decorated by rubbing, stamping or stenciling shapes with geometric borders and repeated motifs of fish or leaf figures in the center. The natural dyes are usually black or rust-browns of various shades. I knew the Tapa cloth was significant in some way, then found out the cloth (known as *masi* in Fiji) is usually worn on formal occasions. It is highly prized for its decorative value and is often found hung on walls as decoration, used as room dividers, and may be used as a blanket. The Fijians also use the masi to wrap sacred objects and is traditionally exchanged as a gift during events like marriages and funerals; if the Tapa was given to them by a chief, or even the royal family, it is more valuable. As I curiously watched the crone women dance in unison, I noticed their faces showed no expression. I understand they take their rituals very seriously and do not allow emotion to alter the ritual.

Holy Cow! I was witnessing actual tribal customs! This was not a cultural show put on for tourists, but a true ethnic celebration! Could these be dances from descendants of Mo'ikeha or Hotu Matu'a Gods? I looked around me and I was surrounded in the experience; drummers and dancers circled around the center, as villagers circled around them. The Fijian spirit of community was rich with textures of sensational sounds and a sense of true happiness. I found Fijians to be musically talented, with a passion to sing.

As all this was going on, I kept winking smiles to Mike and whispering to Mary that I couldn't believe we were having a "National Geographic" experience! What was the likelihood of showing up unexpected in a Fijian village and witnessing such tribal customs?

How serendipitous the way this day had started, I thought. I found it "peculiar" that our first driver never showed up and then we were delayed, missing our bus stop. The Universe offered divine right timing, indeed! We ended up in sweet Mita's village for the night as welcomed guests. I'll never forget Mike's insistence and determination that led to our improbable experience.

As the chief presented the ceremonial grog to the Olympians, the Fijian children sitting behind Mary and me got impatient and started gently poking us, then laughing. I turned around and quietly asked their names in English and they responded with full smiles. I was surprised to find the younger generation being exposed to English in school (probably thanks to Bertie). I asked one of the little girls behind me to sing one of her favorite songs, which she did in a low tone. She had gorgeous deep-brown eyes which radiated through her dark-skinned complexion. The girl's healthy eyes and soul reflected the story of her upbringing – a simple life with plant-based foods, schooling and unconditional love from their communal families. The village seemed to be full of happy children, skinny dogs, chickens freely pecking at the ground, with a few spotted goats, all living harmoniously together. The moms, dads, brothers, and aunts were genuinely enjoying the celebration as well. As we walked about the village, the villagers acknowledged us by saying, "Bula – Vinaca!" (hello and welcome).

Now, a few decades later, as I recall that once-of-a-lifetime experience, it harbors a place of reverence inside me. How rich and meaningful the Fijian ceremony was for me. In hindsight now, I understand how embedded their traditions were and how the experience became sacred knowledge for me to witness. The celebration was in its purest impromptu form, untarnished by any "tourist" performance. My exclusive memory may be fading like an aged photograph, but that day and the feelings it left behind will be with me forever!

After the ceremonial festivities, our group was led back to the chief's hut where they offered us bowls of food. We sat on a large grass mat in the center of the floor and ate with our hands "It makes the food taste better," we were told. The meal consisted of savaka (white potato), spiced corned beef, some root vegetable and water. It didn't matter what they served us; it was getting dark and we were all famished from the long day. Fijian tradition always serves their guests first. Bertie and his family joined in the meal a little later. It was awkward for me to be waited on, but their grace and tradition were important to them. Not only did it honor us, but reflected their graciousness of spirit.

Our basic needs were met with satisfying food and simple translations. As we finished up our meal, a few of the younger men joined us as the chief started up another session of drinking kava. Since the grog is traditionally drunk by the men late into the evening, two of the village women came in and motioned us gals to step outside. We were led to a thatched hut across the way and shown where the outhouse was (a corrugated tin enclosure with no roof). The dirt floor in our sleeping hut was covered with many handmade grass mats, from the leaves of the Pandanus tree. We laid our sarongs down over the padded mats for our sleeping spots. As I laid my tired head down, I felt nothing less than emotional gratitude for the nourishing meal they had provided us as I surrendered to sweet abandon.

We felt embraced and accepted to be included in their gathering. I have great admiration for the Fijians now. They lived simply with little in material possessions, but offered us what they had. I recall lightly waking several times during the night and I could hear the men chanting their ancient songs only a hut away. I smiled and floated back to my unreal dreams.

When daylight came and the roosters began crowing, my eyes slowly focused on the beautiful handiwork around me. The warming light reflected woven bamboo walls while I noticed high overhead, like fine artwork, the intricate patterns and textures of woven palm-thatching. Smiling women offered us rice and fruit for breakfast as we shared our names and were introduced to their young children. I checked in with Mike, who looked a little blurry-eyed. I asked how long they had stayed up with the men. He had no idea, but said that he had had an unforgettable experience. I gave him a big G'day hug and said, "Good on ya."

Mike had asked permission to stay another day, while Bertie and friends made plans to take us to their beach and show us their village lands. Mike, who had become our group leader, had purchased some rice and food from their small roadside market to contribute to lunch and that evening's dinner. We took off by foot for our day's adventure with ten of the village men and boys. A few spoke English, but they mostly communicated in their native Fijian tongue or used hand signals.

As a young woman, hanging out with a group of half-naked Fijian men for the day would rate as another highlight, no doubt. The Fijian DNA has passed along their strong muscular stature. The men wore no shirts, no shoes, just their traditional *sulus* and their warm white smiles. The sulu resembles a skirt and is commonly worn both by men and women. Even Mike and Dan were sporting sulus over their board shorts that day. We women had been sleeping and playing in our sulus already for several days; for some reason, being a minimalist came easy for me.

Bertie took us first past his hut on the hill and brought a horse down from his land; being the gentleman he was, he offered it to the "gals." Lori and Mary jumped on bareback, as I walked with the guys down the dusty dirt road. The passing terrain was dominated by open savannas of tall grasses as distant palms swayed in the coastal breeze. We were quite the cast of characters walking down that road; six Yanks interspersed with the islanders that could be traced back to ancient Polynesian tribes. Along the way, we stopped near Bertie's uncle's property and had a climbing demonstration of the coconut palms. The young men made it look incredibly easy wrapping their wide feet around the tall leaning palms and shimmying up with their arms and legs with machetes tied to their hips to use to cut down the coconuts. We laughed when Dan, with his strong surfing limbs, made it three-quarters of the way up a palm.

The gals shared a coconut full of fresh, wonderfully satisfying coconut water; I could feel my body rehydrating instantaneously. The noonday heat of the day and a long walk on the dusty road had become almost unbearable. I tried to push away the exhaustion with anticipation of the beach just ahead. We arrived with great relief almost forty-five minutes later. Just a little disappointed to find the water not cool nor deep enough to swim in. The sandy reef extended another five-hundred feet to the coral reef beyond. But it was wonderfully wet, as I collapsed right there in the thigh-deep water.

The island men showed us a game called "nei" which was played with a whole coconut and passed to each other in rapid succession, similar to the game 'hot potato,' but over the water's edge. When you missed your catch, the coconut splashed in your face and everyone laughed at you. The game gave us a good workout as we leaped, jumped and splashed while bar-b-qued lamb and roots were cooked on an open pit nearby. Not quite a feast, but satisfying nourishment.

After lunch, we set off for another hike. Bertie wanted to show us the nearby river. We walked until the dirt road intersected with another road and were glad when an old truck came by and the men flagged it down. We all piled into the dusty truck-bed and caught a ride directly to the river, probably another two miles ahead. Once again, I was surprised there was no swimming hole; the river had a decent flow over small volcanic rocks and was colder than the ocean. We sat near the river's edge and soaked our hot dusty feet and enjoyed a reprieve under the shade trees. Bertie started calling us back together for the hour-long hike back to the village. As we walked back, I remember having a conversation with Bertie about the ceremonial grog and why the men stay up all night long. He mentioned that it was routine for ovulating women to send their men off to drink for the night because when they returned they would be unable to "get it up." *How smart*, I thought, *for a natural birth control method.*

We arrived back all steamy and hot after the long walk to the roadside village store. Mike asked for donations from our group, then proceeded to buy frozen orange ice blocks (popsicles) for all the villagers who had accompanied us on our adventure. Smiles and appreciation were exchanged by all. It was a good day to be in Draniv-i-Ra.

We were invited back to the chief's bure for dinner that evening. This time, as I stepped into the family home, I felt a connection to the chief's family, to the community, and became acutely aware of each detail in the room. I remember the blue painted room with open shuttered windows as the cotton-flowered curtains gently danced in the breeze. We all sat in a circle on the floor mats, and I had a partial view through the two open windows of the distant lacey-white reef edge. A sense of emotional gratitude filled me. The serving bowls and wooden servers were hand-carved. Everyone wore colorful sulus and the movement of service brought vitality into the room. Every action I witnessed was a gift received.

We were initially served rice with a light curry sauce. The tangible sensation of using a banana leaf as your plate in one hand, while shoveling delectable flavors into your mouth with your fingers, felt primitive and natural. The next course consisted of spinach and corned-beef baked in coconut milk . . . *oh, so tasty.* I was told the dish originated from Samoa, called Palusami. Palusami – baked parcels of taro leaves enclosing a coconut cream, onion and some type of meat or seafood filling. Taro leaves contain calcium oxalate with some varieties possessing a considerable "bite," but most of the "bite" was removed by cooking.

The last dish they offered was an exquisite stuffed crab, cooked with coconut milk and local herbs. Our last feast together, at least for me, was bathed in sacred ambiance. When you sense gratitude in the moment, your ego steps aside, allowing you to enjoy greater love and understanding. We became an extended family, if only for a few days or hours, but my heart was deeply touched forever. I treasured it then and ever after!

After we finished our meal, we stepped outside and enjoyed the evening moonlight by interacting with Bertie's two young children. His wife did not speak English, so Bertie interpreted her messages of traditions and how life is changing in the village. Bertie and his family excused themselves by walking us down towards the "community" hut where we enjoyed our last ceremonial grog circle; clapping and laughing always ensued. The gals and I left after two rounds and found our sleeping place laid out with mats in the nearby hut. Falling asleep came easily after this wonderful day of heat and hiking. Again, I heard the sounds of the men singing from that deep place inside their chests, coming up through history, through their hearts, surrounding everyone within earshot like a cozy blanket.

When we left the following morning, it seemed like half the village walked us down towards the main road; others waved with their big smiles saying, "Samotha" (goodbye). I felt that familiar sadness in my heart again, as I did when leaving my family back in the states, or leaving Abe behind. It was with such unselfishness that they shared their lives with us for two days; their customs and generosity have stayed with me all these many years.

I now recall that day, some thirty years later, with such appreciation and wonder. It was one of the greatest experiences of my life! We were not seen as tourists with money. We became connected due of our genuine interest to experience village life for a few days. In that experience, we shared the joy and laughter of simply being human. I know now that it was all about timing; having met Mike at the right moment, at the right place, on the right day. Without that connection, I would have been sitting in a dive resort having a staged "island performance" instead. Draniv-i-Ra touched my soul deeply. There is also some regret when I remember Bertie and his village – I had a mailing address, but never sent a "thank-you" note. I recall seeing Mike and Phil a year later while visiting the Mt. Rose Ski resort and felt better when Mike told me he had sent back photos of our days in Dranivi-i-Ra.

CHAPTER 11

Over three hundred islands make up Fiji, with a rich mixture of Melanesians, Indians, Polynesians, Micronesians, Chinese, and Europeans. Early sugar production made way for foreign tourism and Fiji's coral reefs are revered by divers around the world. The group of islands are arrayed in a horseshoe configuration and enclose the Koro Sea. Of the three hundred or so islands, only one hundred and six have been deemed large enough to inhabit. That leaves approximately two hundred uninhabited islands that are either too small, too isolated, or don't have enough fresh water to sustain people. I found it interesting that Captain James Cook, who sailed the Pacific between 1768 and 1779 in largely uncharted territory, found the Polynesians to be more 'ocean dwellers' than land mammals.

Nananu-i-Ra Island, March 30th

For the past four days, I've been on a deserted island called Nananu-i-Ra. I returned to Sunseekers Lodge for a night to repack my gear and get situated before striking out on my own. I took the local bus back towards Raki-Raki along the Kings Road, winding past Viti Levu Bay towards the northern-most tip of the island. Destination: the Ellington Wharf for a boat trip to Nananu-i-Ra Island, a fifteen minute ride over clear calm waters.

Lonely Planet had informed me the island was deserted except for some basic bungalows. I knew I needed to bring my own food supplies so I stopped in a convenience store as I walked down towards the dock. I picked up some basics like packaged pasta, can of tomato sauce, granola, powdered milk and some fruit. I knew next to nothing about the island other than there was no road or villages and that accommodations were basic. Charlie's Place offered basic bungalows (approximately 2 or 3) with limited power by generator in the evening hours. A composting toilet and cold shower were offered in each bungalow. I found a two bedroom bungalow available to share with a couple from Sweden.

Nananu-i-Ra is a small 3.5 km triangular island with scalloped bays and amber sand beaches ideal for snorkeling and diving. The name of the island means "Daydream of the West" and as soon as I arrived, the image of tranquil rest and relaxation became a welcomed reality.

A refreshing breeze caressed my bare shoulders and outstretched arms as I sat swinging in a saggy hammock. Behind me, a luscious wall of jungle greenery contained my stark beach as I swung under the tall shade palms. I heard birds loudly shrieking throughout the jungle canopy. As I swayed, floating above the earth suspended in time, I was soothed by the gently lapping waters radiating warmth. Uninhibited freedom overwhelmed me as the sun dropped nonchalantly behind a flat horizon. *Was it just my imagination?* Or was I truly *here* – alone on a forgotten beach cradled in a hammock, peeking through the cotton mesh at my sand-flecked toes?

Then, like a spontaneous eruption from deep inside, a giddy and full-bodied laugh of joy bellowed . . . *Haaaa Haaaaa Haaaa Heeeeeeee*! I felt the vastness of time and space, realizing I was similar to a small speck of sand on this tiny atoll scattered among the thousands in the vast Pacific. It was a huge leap of faith to recognize what I had created at this moment; No grand finale. No friends to high-five my success. Friends and family back home could *never* actually fathom where I was at this moment or how many miles, actually weeks, I had traveled to arrive at my new state of self-imposed emptiness! Alone in my quiet awareness, thoughts flashed between breaths of memories, giddy laughter and the perfection of NOW, where the soft breeze scratched the palms to and fro above my head.

My white-washed stucco cabin with glass-louvered windows sat just steps away from the turquoise sea. Knowing I had nowhere to go for the next week, I felt nothing less than complacent. In that dreamlike state, I was satisfied with my plan; with enough food and water to last me until the boat returned the following week. My strategy, if I had any at that point, was to spend my days leisurely combing the remote beach, snorkeling lovely coral gardens, writing and just emptying my mind of analysis. Suspended in the essence of life, enjoying what each moment offered. And IT was more than enough!

Lethargy was good for me; thank goodness "guilt" is not a part of my vocabulary. There was nothing to do but lounge on my tropical beach or go swimming. I explored the length of the beach and wished I could hike into the interior of the island (or to the other side of the island), but the vegetation was intimidating – who knows what bugs and reptiles existed in that dense thicket.

Once the rain started that night, I barely moved from my bed and it might as well just be noon. I was bored – not from being on the island, but being stuck inside. My instant food sustained me, but lacked appeal and I found myself daydreaming of my next destination: Beachcomber Island, an all-inclusive resort complete with daily buffets to delight my every whim.

My last night on Nananu-i-Ra had an unexpected surprise. A Dutch man, down the beach in another bungalow, caught his biggest fish yet (a Bluestripe Snapper) and shared it with my bungalow-mates and me. They cooked it up with rice and lentils and it tasted divine, eating something fresh with a squeeze of lime.

Looking back on these last days of detachment, I loathed the idea of going back to scummy Nadi to catch another boat to Beachcomber. *This* was pure paradise on my scale of tropical experiences. Steps from my bungalow stretched the golden sand and warm turquoise waters. Snorkeling offered a brilliant array of fish: I came face-to-face with schools of brilliant Blue Tangs, a corny-looking Pufferfish and several good-sized Blueface Angels (with dynamic colors of deep blue scales, trimmed in bright chartreuse, creating an intricate glowing lattice affect; Angels also have a bright yellow dorsal fin, accented with a deep blue dot, and a yellowish mask covering their noses and mouths around a blue face).

When you're swimming among these intricately designed fish, you know the creator had a vivid imagination or a great sense of humor. There were many schools of Zebra Dart fish and when I saw the large black and white Sergeant Majors, I shouted with such excitement that I accidently spit out my snorkel. The brilliant small blue Damsels with yellow bottoms were stunning and I was surprised by the size of a very curious Squaretail Coral Grouper.

After a full day of fun in the ocean, I later had difficulty trying to sleep in the evening with no breeze, no fan. It was stifling and muggy. The crickets outside sounded like a choir and the few scurrying cockroaches inside were huge. I was tired of my dang sinus cold hanging-on while living in the tropics. I also had a small puncture wound on the bottom of one foot that showed beginning signs of an infection. Just when I was beginning to think life is perfect, I found myself feeling drained and grumpy that evening, living in my paradisaic dream. *Guess I should pull the sheet up over my head to keep the flying cockroaches from landing on me in the night, as I sleep off my bad attitude.*

After Beachcomber Island, April 5

Beachcomber Island was all I expected, and less. A shuttle boat picked me up from Nadi Harbor, some eleven miles to the island. I booked myself into a dorm room with bunks, fabric dividers for privacy and community toilets and showers.

I didn't realize that the island was Ausi-land's favorite "party" island destination. Thank God, my lifesavers showed up the second day I was there. Unbeknownst to me, Mike and Phil walked off a shuttle boat with their big friendly smiles aglow. It was wonderful to have my Yankee drinking mates for the next three days of palling-around. We saw plenty of sunshine, a little rain, endless booze, dancing and tons of snorkeling!

One sunset evening, I took a walk around the entire island by myself. It took me a little over an hour – that's how small this sandy reef is. The first evening's entertainment was lovely Polynesian Hula dancers. On Wednesday night, a group of Fijians arrived and performed their harmonizing island songs and dance. Except for the traveling entertainment, which rotated from island-to-island resort on different days of the week, the regular late evening musician, whom we nicknamed "Barry" (for Manilow), strummed his guitar and sang standard Neil Diamond and other American pop songs. Over the consecutive nights, we weren't sure if Barry was sounding better or if he just kept pulling out different songs from his repertoire.

The guys and I took a glass bottom boat out that first morning, which gave me a directional bearing for later coral diving. The underworld beauty inspires with different shapes, color and depth of coral. It's no wonder Fiji is known for its barrier reefs, as the great Koro Sea off the north coast comprises the fourth longest reef in the world and, no doubt, the most colorful. We had Blue Chromis fish erupting in excitement as we threw white bread overboard; some were eager enough to jump up out of the water.

I went out snorkeling several times each day after that boat ride. I got to look a multi-colored Parrot Fish in the eye; saw a Fire Clownfish, brightly cinnamon-colored with a large white stripe; and saw a comical Longhorn Cowfish, colored in pale yellow bearing blue spots with two pairs of long horns and a pair of prominent lips with a fluttering translucent top fin. I could part the waters, suffice to speak, as I swam through schools of yellow fish, speckled with electric cerulean blue and indigos. The bigger the fish, the more nervous I got when they came curiously close to my toes!

My favorite fish to swim with were the stunning Scribbled Angelfish, some almost eleven inches long, predominately a dark blue-black fish with bright yellow lips, and a wide vertical band of yellow separating the head and top fin with yellow tails. I even spotted "Dory" (from *Finding Nemo*) the stunning Pacific Blue Tang, or a Palette Surgeonfish, showing bright blue with yellow tails.

"If there is magic on this planet, it is contained in water."
Loren Eiseley

******

Since Fiji is to Aussies what Hawaii is to the Yanks, I felt, at times, like I was visiting Australia without going there – the accents were thick and slurred. I understood why the obnoxiously drunk twenty-year old twerps were there – duh, all drinks were included in the all-inclusive package and, we know, Aussies love to drink! I felt lucky to have Mike and Phil to kick around with and protect me from the Aussies' insufferable juvenile displays. All we could do was laugh *at them* together; when they thought we were laughing *with them*.

After the third full day on the island, I realized that the "all-you-can-eat" buffets were the same food, day after day. Dinners consisted of corned beef, rice and potatoes; breakfasts offered granola, yogurt, very little fruit and scrambled eggs. It was tolerable, but I half-expected to have an abundant serving of tropical fruits and fish.

On my last evening on the island, I celebrated with Mike, Phil and some more-mature Aussies and their girlfriends. What an opportunity it had been to meet 'the boys' and experience our Fijian village together – we would always be 'connected' by that thread of cultural understanding. So, like brothers and sisters, we danced and we toasted Malibu (rum) and O.J.s late into the night.

CHAPTER 12

Plantation Island

Moving onward to the next adventure, I left my buds behind on Beachcomber as I proceeded to Plantation Island Resort. For $30, I was able to take a 10-seater plane from the mainland to Plantation. Once seated in the prop-plane, I realized the wing propellers were my only view outside the window. It was a smooth takeoff and a not-too-nerve-racking 15-minute flight, but then I noticed the landing strip below was gravel and grass. I squinted as we neared the ground, and as we rolled to a bumpy stop, I finally exhaled. All passengers were greeted by a smiling Fijian man who chauffeured us in a pull-tractor to the lobby.

I was glad my first impression of Plantation Island was wrong. The funky tractor and the airport wooden bench left me wondering what my accommodations would be like. But, I was impressed with my modern dorm room with lounges full of soft chairs, a nicely furnished bar and restaurant, a deluxe swimming pool and a video room. Windsurfing was available, as were water skiing and paddle boards. The only drawback to Plantation Island was that the resort charged extra for meals and drinks – which meant less drinking, which was probably a good thing, though maybe not as fun.

Since Plantation Island is a bit upscale, I noticed it attracted more of the honeymoon-type guests, which only reminded me of my boyfriend back home. I was starting to look forward to going home soon, and began to feel blue one evening watching the lovey-dovey couples. Then I met a woman, Karen, that first evening, who coincidentally happened to be originally from Santa Cruz (with her dad being a partner in a prominent CPA firm)! We had an interesting conversation about relationships with men as she shared her similar story about a deep connection with a man back in California, and a relationship with an Australian. We both agreed that romantic magic can happen quickly, but how do you sustain that connection? I mean, there is no way *one* person can be the right person for you. In a world so big with so many people . . . perhaps it's about timing, that's all.

While on Plantation Island, I made company with two sisters from Boston and a guy from Canada, then got side-swiped as soon as I met Colin on a snorkeling trip. I noticed his handsome good looks, but I was too shy to engage him 'til he saw me at the bar that evening and sat down next to me. The next day, he joined me as I shared some tips on windsurfing in an impromptu lesson. One thing led to another – by the end of the day we were sharing a bottle of wine over a romantic dinner. As brief as our time together would be, I was curious to hear his stories: Colin was born and raised in Sydney, traveled through Asia, Malaysia, Bangkok, the Himalayas, and he even spent seven years in San Diego working for NCR Corporation (banking industry), which now had him stationed in Norway.

How exciting! I thought, *to have seen so much.* But, in a way, there was a quiet loneliness about him, too.

I figured I was safe from his romantic gestures as we were both staying in separate dorm rooms. Not so . . . as I followed him down the dimming trail after dinner, headed towards the dirt airport landing-strip. The wooden airport "waiting" bench was put to new use that evening as Colin "shot me to the stars" with his master, tongue technics . . . and my young flower became his textbook! His passion in pleasing me superseded the annoying symphony of whining mosquitoes. I laugh remembering that moment now – safe sex at the airport reef with the added reminder of itchy bites that plagued me the following week. *But it was worth it!*

The third morning on Plantation, I went with the Boston sisters on a snorkeling trip to a nearby wreck – a sunken sailboat from the 60's that had grown colorful coral. The dives were as exhilarating as imagined . . . the sensation of the primeval seas speaks to my soul! The touch of the warm, amniotic water on my skin is like a sensuous soft, close embrace, floating me into eternal ecstasy. Adding to my all-encompassing sensory experience, the sealife offered another dimension to that awe. I saw more amazing and unusual tropical fish than I'd yet seen: from Parrotfish to the blue-yellow-striped Clown Loaches. There were large yellow jet-black Angel fish that made me almost howl under water! And when I touched the exotic lips of a large Blue-lipped Clam, I hummed! Only those who have experienced the fluidity of free diving can understand I was IN "cloud nine." The coral reefs that exist in the South Seas are some of the best in the entire world. I witnessed coral reefs in colors of deep purples to the Carnation Corals colored in maroon tucked under a rock; there were bleached and blushed Finger Leather hard corals that said, "stay back." Ever seen a Tongue Coral wiggle at you? I did! I also spotted large green Plate Corals gathered along a swath of giant rocks. Simply astounding!

The rest of the day, I hung along the white-sand beach at the resort windsurfing or paddling around on a paddleboard. Not realizing how quickly the weather can change as clouds started to form overhead, I spent my last hours in the water while it rained down on me – as comfortable as a child in a warm bath, floating in the shoreline. I could pack all the fun in a backpack, but the best of me could not, would not, be contained!

Few regrets now . . . when I think of how much I was enjoying myself, I never stopped to take photos – so the reminders of Plantation Island now only exist in my memories. Was I too lazy to take photos, or was I truly living in the moment? Murphy's Law, of course, the next day . . . rain and the vivid beauty had become washed in grey.

All and all, I loved Plantation Island due to its spaciousness, compared to Beachcomber. I attempted to walk the entire island one afternoon – which I was told would take two hours to circumvent – but I collected too many shells and felt hungry before I made it half way around. I'll also remember the first night's sunset which happened too quickly to photograph, but had postcard Technicolor written all over it.

Departing Fiji, April 9

After four days on Plantation Island, I had no problem reaching level "ten" of relaxation. Never had to worry about a thing until that last day trying to get off the island as a storm approached and I was concerned about making my next connecting flight in Nadi. Instead of worrying too much, I made early morning arrangements for the first boat off the island since they could not guarantee the safety of planes with oncoming winds and storm. So, there I was, sitting in Nadi airport, waiting for my two-hours "behind schedule" flight to Rarotonga, Cook Islands. I had time to reflect on my beautiful memories in Fiji and the marvel of their world-class reefs.

CHAPTER 13

Rarotonga, Cook Islands – April 10

Rarotonga Island is known as the jewel of the Pacific, with stunning sawtooth peaks and lush jungle slopes covered in flamboyant exotic trees. Everything one would fantasize about if you could escape to an ideal castaway dream would be found on the Cook Islands!

My flight, via Air New Zealand initiated in Auckland, stopped in Nadi, Fiji for refueling before the 1,500 mile island hop to Rarotonga. I believed it was well over nine hours before I'd land. We departed in early evening, so we would be flying most of the night and arriving at daybreak. I attempted to sleep but was too excited to be finishing up the last leg of my trip and exploring the last of the archipelago islands.

With no less than a wink and a nod, I found myself walking the aisles in the middle of the night. As I neared the cockpit on one of my rounds, the captain's door was open and a stewardess was crouched inside looking up through the windshield. The gal stood up excitedly and asked if I wanted to see Halley's Comet. I had heard that Halley's apparition had started mid-March, but never thought that *I* would see it. I squatted down between the pilot and co-pilot as one of them pointed up into the dark expanse. Even though we were fortunate to be 2,000 feet up in the sky in one of the most remote territories on earth, the tiny snowball being tossed through the heavens was disappointing. I did, in fact, see it faintly with my bare eyes, and will probably never have an opportunity to see it again in my lifetime. It returns every 75 years or so: Next showing 2061! I learned a few fun facts from the pilot, who noted that Halley's Comet has one of the highest velocities relative to the Earth of any object in the Solar System. He also surprised me with the fact that the earliest documented sighting was in 240 B.C.

******

The moment we landed and I stepped onto Rarotonga Island, I fell into a trance state. The energy on the island is so far removed from the push of the modern world – I felt like I'd stepped into another dimension of time. The aquamarine lagoons could be filled with angelic mermaids softly whispering my name. *Quite possibly . . . maybe?*

My accommodations were recommended by a friend back in California, who suggested I use one of my layovers to visit the Cook Islands. Sally's Arorangi Lodge was located in one of the five districts that make up Rarotonga situated on the west coast of the island. I met Sally right away and she introduced me to her eight-room wooden lodge and set me up with an upstairs room to be shared with an older woman named Marlene. Sally had an available motor scooter that she would also rent to me for an additional $9 a day.

The island was formed by a large volcano, which now sits dormant and is nearly thirty-miles in diameter, with a coastal road skirting the island. The island is surrounded by white-sanded lagoons, which often extend more than three-hundred feet to the outer reef, then steeply slide into the deep, deep blue. Unfortunately, most of the lagoons are too shallow for swimming or for snorkeling, but I planned to explore a lagoon to the southeast called Muri Beach that was said to be wide and deep enough for snorkeling.

As I walked down along the lagoon behind Sally's lodge, I found myself collecting unusual seashells – I found one of the largest spiral shells I'd ever held! I reached for the small shells and bleached corals as well, to feel their contours and imagine how they grew. I'd rotate and hold them in such a way to get sunlight to reflect into their crevices so I could gain insight, not only into the shape of the object, but its overall form, its third dimension.

Most of the interior of the island is dominated by eroded volcanic pinnacles choked in dense vegetation, remaining unpopulated due to its foreboding terrain. The beauty and majesty of the razorback ridges and jutting peaks took my breath away, once I reminded myself to look up.

I had a fulfilling day, zipping around the island on my scooter, my destination . . . Muri Beach. It was a treat to be on my own to explore or stop anywhere I chose. I got distracted once or twice, stopping to explore an old church, a nearby graveyard, and a foot trail into the jungle.

That afternoon, I found Muri Beach barren of people and enjoyed a serene walk along the beach looking for treasures.

I found myself thinking about the end of this trip and what might happen once I returned home – I had to remind myself to focus on where I was! *I was on one of the world's more remote islands – in the center of the world!* As I walked Muri Beach that day, how could I fathom that this place would be transformed into a recreational haven for activities like scuba diving and deep-sea fishing, kite surfing and horseback riding, as the almighty tourist dollar would change this paradise forever in the next decade. I understand that this tranquil beach now holds the Muri Beach Club Hotel, which can accommodate you for a mere $500 NZ/night for an all-inclusive destination experience! What was once *not* there, will never be again!

As I headed back to my parked scooter, I noticed an open door to the demure-wooden Muri Beach Sailing Club. I stepped inside and found two salty locals propping up one end of the bar, so I stepped up to the other end asking for a cold Steinlager. It was so refreshing, being back in New Zealand territory with the familiar Kiwi dollars and a higher quality of food being shipped from Auckland. As soon as I found out they served green-lipped mussels from the mainland, I immediately placed an order! If I could take one moment out of time and replay it over and over, it would be slurping green-lipped mussels savoring their briny taste as I chased down a cold Steinie, while sitting looking out over the empty Muri Beach Lagoon. I felt right at home at this "local" hangout as the only tourist around.

> *I have never found the companion that was so companionable as solitude.*
> Henry David Thoreau

Saturday, April 12

Sliding into the island pace . . . I'm cherishing my unscheduled life as much as possible. The hardest thing I think I've done since I've been here is trying to get my motor scooter lifted up and over the bloody kick stand. I've put a small gash in my shin already.

My first evening, I scootered twelve minutes over to the District of Avarua, just north of my lodge. Avarua is the epicenter of the island, with the harbor and airport nearby. Avarua has a cabaret, some discos, several restaurants as well as a selection of cafés and bars. I had heard about the notorious Banana Court and was hungry for food, drink and a little excitement. I found the drinks were cheap and strong and there was a pleasant outside verandah offering a view of the harbor. By the time I finished my second rum drink, all inhibitions had vanished and I found myself moving freely through the bar making conversation with various travelers. By disco hour, I was in rare form and dancing just to sweat-out all the alcohol I had consumed. My memory of that night is vague; I don't recall dancing on the tables or having sex in the parking lot, but I *do* remember riding my scooter home in my little sun dress. By midnight, the air was still warm as it gently brushed my bare arms and legs. I had the sensation of flying through the dark as my hair twisted around my head and my eyes watered from the speed. It was obviously late, as I saw no other vehicles on that two-lane road. I was alone in the night with my one headlight beaming into the darkness and the expansive cosmos guiding me from above.

*Loneliness adds beauty to life. It puts a special burn on
sunsets and makes Night air smell better.*

Henry Rollins

On the second night, I had an arranged dinner and cultural
show with my roommate, Marlene, and her new friends, Kathy
and Len, for company. The dinner was presented in traditional
island feast style with their delicacy – grilled mahi-mahi over
coconut rice, baked potatoes or roots cooked in-ground, called
umu kai. We ate our meals accompanied by colorful dancing
and drumming. The choreographed dancers were decorated
with fresh tropical flowers. Those flowers were beautiful, but
I became hypnotized by the male Hula dancers and their
dark sinewy chests.

Afterwards, we hit the classy Outrigger Restaurant for a drink
and were surprised by the somewhat impromptu cabaret-like
show. To our amazement, the local transvestites were decked-
out in their finest flash of jewelry, eyelashes and padded bras.
They were having a roaring good time drinking at the bar
near the front of the restaurant, creating a unique "social"
scene. I was delighted to see the island had a place where
they could hang-out and be accepted for who they were. They
laughed, teased, and sang with ukulele accompaniment. Was
it part show or was it real? I'll never know, but I recall my
face hurting after smiling so hard that evening! Not sure if I
was laughing or just astonished by their antics.

Another blissful scooter ride home that night . . . something
about the slowness, the warm darkness, and the feeling of

pure joy and freedom . . . my senses were heightened by the darkness; the breeze on my bare skin and the smell of the perfumed tropical air contributed to my peace.

Kathy and I seemed to hit it off the night before. She, too, was finishing up her trip after a bicycle tour of Australia and New Zealand, with her bicycle already shipped home to Washington State. We came up with a plan to visit Atuitaki Island together within the coming days. Since we were of similar mind and it was getting dark on a Saturday night, what else is there to do while visiting Avarua? Definitely not play Solitaire in your room. As partners-in-crime this time, we scootered back down to the Banana Court for a wild and flirty good stretch of the evening.

The one experience "you should not miss," as recommended in my Lonely Planet guide, was that you attend a Sunday church service in one of the district's white-washed churches. The following morning, I took off after a quick breakfast and headed south along the coast road with a daypack full of beach gear, in search of a church. I came across Titikaveka District and saw many scooters parked outside of their church. As I walked slowly up the church path, I could hear the harmonized voices from inside and was pulled magnetically through the front doors. It seemed the locals had turned out in their Sunday best with the women dressed immaculately in their bright flowery dresses and their stiff *rito* hats made of coconut fiber.

Most of the service was in their native language, but it was the singing . . . oh, the singing, that captured my heart! I was just a bystander sitting on the back bench, enthralled!

There were about a dozen men and women up front, leading the small congregation in song. I wish I would have known some of the native tongue, but then maybe that's what made it so exotic and beautiful. I felt invisible sitting in the back, but not alone; a few large women turned and smiled and I smiled in return.

The singing tones reminded me of African Soweto songs; so primal, from their roots. I was later told, "They sing to open their souls and their hearts." I know that is how my heart felt . . . songs that make you vulnerable to your own emotions. Their harmonies tenderized me, softened me and inflated my essence. If the transvestites didn't open my mind the night before, my heart was blown wide open with love, listening to their singing . . . getting into the hidden cracks of my being. Meeting together on the *"same page, in creation, in hardship, in silence and out loud."* As my favorite author, Anne Lamott, continues:

"The harmonies were round, had solidity, without interpreta-tion, so spirit came out big and solid. There was no piano, so people tuned into one another's voices, and their sound was strong and assured, but also had a great brightness and glitter. The channel was from deep down inside the earth; it came up through the crust, to the ground, and up through our feet and up through our chests and hearts and up our throats and out of our mouths... and it somehow also rose through the air, to the sky, to the stars, this sound that had come up through our rough feet." (Traveling Mercies: Thoughts on Faith (2000))

Thank you, Anne, for succinctly describing my impression of that experience in that Cook Island chapel.

****

Now, it was my last day on the island and all of life had flowed in perfect rhythm – positively slow. Rarotonga moved at its own pace; the people there are casual and friendly. I believe one of the main attractions about the Cooks is that it is a REAL place, not manufactured for tourism (at least back then). Real islanders still live there and deal with all the problems that tiny islands face trying to cope with a modern world that is growing around it. In a world of instant communication and jet travel, I believe you can find that idyllic place where lost horizons still exist.

That morning I finally made contact with my boyfriend by phone. It felt good to hear his voice and know all was well with my dog, Sadie. Our conversation was brief, but he let me know everything was good. I found myself counting the days 'til I could see his smile and feel his long arms wrapped around me.

Marlene flew to Tahiti last evening, and our little community of friends saw Drew off to Fiji today. Coincidental travelers we had all become, sharing our histories for a short while before being flung out into the Universe again. What a gift getting to know other excursionists like myself, who reflected back interesting aspects of my own life.

CHAPTER 14

Aitutaki Island, April 15

What incredible views I had flying over the Cook Islands after getting a window seat in the ten-seater plane. From my aerial view, I spotted blue-green reefs, turquoise and indigo blue waters in the bleached sand atolls and banks of orange coral just below the ocean's surface. Absolutely the most sublime view of the South Pacific I could have imagined, seeing Mother Earth wearing such a string of exquisite pearls.

The Cook Islands are unquestionably jewels of the highest order. As we came closer to Aitutaki, I spotted the triangular-shaped reef embraced by an aqua lagoon in which nested twelve small coral islands. I knew Aitutaki had very little in the way of supplies, but it didn't matter at this point. I'd gotten by so far on this trip with intuition and determination. Who needs food? Being in the moment was all that mattered. Sustenance would be made available.

The flight to Aitutaki with Kathy was, no doubt, the most enjoyable airlift I have ever had; a hop, skip and a 40-minute jump to the northern Cooks. Along for the ride, the male friend Marlene had introduced us to, Len, was on the same plane. Within an hour, we landed on a WWII airstrip and were left to fend for ourselves. It took us another hour to ask around for whatever accommodations could be found on the small island. It was a cross between a tiny hotel with one room, fridge and 3 beds, or a two-bedroom plywood house. Len, Kathy and I decided to share the house, which had a western view and a short, sandy strip of beach. Due to the shallow reef, we didn't have a swimming beach, but one could see the white-laced waves rolling 200 feet away.

That evening at sunset, Len and I scootered down to the end of the pier to watch the islanders flyfish. The silhouette of the kids standing on their outriggers, fly-fishing, and the glorious sun dipping behind the clouds made me appreciate how simple and beautiful life is. There was a group of about five horses being washed at the beach by their handlers as the luminescent sunlight silhouetted the palm trees in the foreground; the trees became vivid and dominant in the flawless Pacific sunset. Just one moment of awareness that takes your breath away.

If you want to know how small Aitutaki really is, imagine this . . . within a couple of hours after renting the two-bedroom house, word had spread throughout the island that there was a man with two women living together! When we would go about our day, the islanders already knew that we were that "three-some couple" renting the house.

The island was silent except for an occasional motor scooter buzzing by; a faint goat's bleep could be heard from a nearby neighbor, or a beautiful song floated through the palms from an island bird. Believe it or not, no dogs were heard barking or fighting. (I now realize how Rarotonga was over-run by stray dogs). No dogs were allowed on Aitutaki.

One late afternoon as I sat outside our rental, I noticed an old outrigger canoe with a one-sided float-beam and a single paddle inside. Since it was parked on our beach and no one was around, I pushed it into the shallows and took it out for a spin, feeling lopsided and unbalanced as I stood in its hull. Fish darted below my feet, hovering above the pure white sands.

Pure paradise – what a lovely remote island Aitutaki was back then – probably still is – but I count myself as unusually lucky to have experienced the isolated island before resort inns became scattered along the one road from Arutunga Harbor to the airport, now fetching upwards of $200 per night.

We arranged a lagoon tour with Kathy, Len, and an Australian couple we met, to some of the inner reef islands. The waters were bright turquoise as we headed off to collect coconuts on one island, grab a few clams from another, and then top off our lunch with octopus from another nearby atoll. Our guide, boatman and fisherman named Tu, was a big Maori with a keen sense of humor who took us to a special spot before lunch for an hour of snorkeling in pacifying waters.

I followed behind one of the more peculiar fish that I had seen who had a nose like a horse, a blue stripe over his eyes, and yellow/brown striping coloring its tail. The abundance and variety of marine life was truly astonishing and it appears that each island has their own unique species. I saw numerous sea cucumbers, but it was the giant (four-foot) blue-lipped clams that awed me! Imagine being smiled at by a dazzling set of blue soft lips bursting from a curvilinear shell! Their colors were a mix of vivid blue, turquoise and green with specs of brown/black pigment cells in their tissues.

After snorkeling to our hearts' content, we headed back to our deserted sandbar on Tekopua for a bar-b-que of our delicacies. Lunch was delectable . . . toasted bread, squid, clams, breadfruit and *paws* (greenish-black fruit that tasted so much better than it looked, with mango-banana-citrus flavors). Pacific clouds blew in from the west and rain started falling upon us as we were eating lunch; our spirits were light and silly as we stood in the showers, rinsing the dried salt from our bodies.

I felt primeval, eating with our hands, standing in the rain, while laughing at our circumstances in the middle of our private islet. Spacious views in every direction surrounded our white sand turquoise sea to the horizon and back. No question in my mind, one of the most enchanting places I've ever eaten lunch! The wet chill from the raw air sent me back into the warm ocean bath where I soaked in the shallow sands, floating in utopia.

After a short while, Tu guided us to wade the sandbank to Tapuaetai or, as it's aptly called, One Foot Island, only ten minutes or roughly, two-hundred steps away. One Foot, similarly shaped like a foot, is another small islet near the southeast point of the lagoon with the broadest view of the entire Aitutaki lagoon.* Unimaginable beauty! Tu shared the tale of how the island got its name – something about a father and son stepping on the same foot prints to avoid the chief who forbade fishing there. The father was captured and swore it was only he fishing, while his son was left wandering the island alone after hiding in a tree. It was, by far, an above-average day spending it with Tu. Whether we were swimming with fish, eating fish, or standing in the rain, I felt like a wrinkled prune by the time we returned to our house later that afternoon.

Sad to say, there are now three man-made structures on One Foot Island. The largest is a combination eating area, bar and souvenir shop which doubles as a post office, which stamps tourist's passports. The other two buildings are weekend cabins.

******

Last Week – April 17

I couldn't believe I was down to the last week before this escapade came to an end; not sure if I was relieved or sad. It seemed to be a mixture of both. I especially enjoyed sleeping in this morning, after staying up half past midnight reading my fourth book on this trip. There is nothing better than sitting inside a protected room listening to the variations of rain falling outside. I love falling asleep to the sound of tropical rain, but better yet, the surprise to wake up and see bright sunny days ahead. The temperature seems to remain the same, be it evening, rain or shine.

Finally – it was the end of my trip and my sinuses had cleared! After three long months . . . my first scuba dive in the Cook Islands was arranged! I was committed, but a bit nervous at first, as I kept calming myself down with an intentional deep breath as our little boat took off from Arutunga Harbor. As we glided over the world's most beautiful lagoon of velvet-aqua waters, we headed out beyond the encircled reef 'til the bright white sands dropped off into infinite cobalt blue.

The Aitutaki archipelago chain consists of an area roughly seven miles long. We would be wall diving on the outside reef with the hopes of seeing black coral. After an awkward backwards splash off the boat in my scuba gear, I stabilized not once, but twice, to get my ears to clear. After thirty, forty feet, my breathing became easier as we slowly descended down to ninety feet, drifting with the mild current.

I saw several good-sized fish about twenty feet below me in water through which I could see no bottom! The visibility was unfathomable compared to coastal California and I was surprised that the warm water temps remained the same, either in shallow or in the deeper blue. At one point, feeling confident as I was kicking out on my own, ahead of the rest of the group, a four-foot black Grouper suddenly came from the depths and swam by me a little too close and curious. He was big, almost as big as I was! Once I got over the shock of his size, I quickly turned back to the group for safety. Neil, our Kiwi dive master, made sure I was okay, asking with hand signals.

A few minutes later I relaxed and began breathing normally, then started twirling somersaults enjoying the freedom of my body. The weightless suspension and the ability to go right or left, backwards or forward, up and down at the same time is to be released from the restraints of gravity; you understand for a few moments the third dimension that birds and fish effortlessly move through.

Our group of four divers neared the scaling cliff; I don't remember seeing black coral, but the colorful marine life attached to the rock was a garden of delight. As we slowly ascended, I looked straight up and saw schools of fish back-lit by the sky and could see bursts of wind on the surface forming tiny wavelets. Neil started feeding some smaller fish as we were nearing the surface. He created a frothing excitement in the water as the fish came hounding up to us, begging for more bread. The fish actually came up to my mask, looking directly into my big eyes and schooled around us intently. For a few moments, I became part of the beautiful magical sphere of marine life. What made the moment so endearing was more than the vividness of their colors, but the sheer number of them all turning in unison as though we comprised a single organism!

Once I reached the surface, my tank was lifted off my back, then I was offered a hand to pull me up back into the boat. We discussed some of the fish we spotted, including the rare Achilles Tang, a beautiful full-sized black Sturgeon with unmistakable bright highlights of white markings and a prominent orange patch around the dorsal fin. It was hard to be pulled out of such marvel!

******

Four days and counting . . . those last few days on the Cook Islands seemed to go by slowly for some reason; I'll blame the grey and rainy weather that allowed me to stay inside, reading another book. Kathy and I went down to the upscale Rarotongan Hotel one morning for a big breakfast and an intentional lay in the sun. The wind began blowing so hard that we were sandblasted on the beach, followed by more afternoon clouds. When all else fails, have a few drinks! We sat around the bar for several hours talking to other travelers. I wish I could just be home, instantly! I was closer to home, yet still 4,700 miles from California. I sat and reflected a lot then – the start of my trip seemed like it was eons ago. The good experiences surpassed my expectations, and the bad… oh, just memories that fade over time.

Travel offers the experience and opportunity to meet new people from all over the world, as well as learning to get along in groups. I have a new appreciation for California progressiveness and the good 'ole USA. I had not missed commercialized TV one iota while abroad. There was so much more to do, to see and to visit, keeping myself entertained with new acquaintances I'd meet each day, or the sunsets that decorated each evening.

My last thirty-five hours were spent in lovely Tahiti on its lush mountainous island. I had an unexpected layover, so I went traipsing around looking for the bungalow where Marlene was staying. I got lost walking in a neighborhood, but then personally experienced the French rudeness of Tahitians, who refused to offer any help whatsoever with directions! I did eventually find Marlene, accidentally, as she was walking out of her cabana. Thankfully, I was able to leave my pack for a few hours as we took a last walk together down to a nearby beach that included exotic French women baring beautiful breasts in the glaring sunshine.

It is good to have an end to journey toward; but it is the journey that matters, in the end.

Ursula K. LeGuin

Epilogue

Several friends have asked, "How was your homecoming?" It wasn't actually part of this story, but since they ask…

My boyfriend-back-home, did in fact, pick me up at the San Francisco airport. I received a substantial hug with a rushed kiss, as he picked up my pack and we headed out the automatic doors. Since Ted wasn't aware of my experiences the last three months, there was initial hesitancy in our reunion, but fortunately he was comfortable enough to bluntly ask, "What is that smell you have?" Could it be a cross between sweaty Tahiti, a 15-hour flight, and a cheap body spray I used on the plane? I did, in fact, smell bad. My reunion with my Sadie dog, though, was heartwarming as she excitedly ran around me, not bothered by my smell at all!

Ted welcomed me back to his rented room in a large Victorian house. Shortly, thereafter, I found a house to share on Westside and when my housemate moved a year later, Ted moved into the house and we've been together ever since.

By Ted "releasing" me to go out on my own, I grew into an adventuresome, stronger and confident person! Our Love has lasted the long run by allowing each other to live our independent joys and passions… be it separate diving, fishing and windsurfing trips, yoga retreats to Mexico and SE Asia, or backpacking alone in the wilderness.

There is no doubt our relationship was sparked by the intrigue of travel. We agreed early on that part of our union would include separate vacations. Don't get me wrong, we love traveling together; I'm lucky to have found a man who travels well. I have girlfriends, I've been told, who live with dependent spouses who would not know what to do without them. Ted and I have found great ryhthm traveling together, when we're at our best, whether we're primitive camping in Utah or busing through Central America.

I have found that when I am on a solo trip or backpacking with a girlfriend, the positive energy I bring back to share with my loved ones enlightens the spark in my eyes! In the routine of our daily lives, it's easy to lose touch with one's free and fun-loving self (especially in a long-term relationship or when being a parent). It's healthy and vital to have time away and not feel guilty about it. It's also crucial to have time to hang out without having to meet anyone's needs but your own.

Loneliness is the poverty of self;
solitude is the richness of self.

May Sarton

Acknowledgments

My first writings were published in the *Goddess Circle News*, circa 1999 – 2017, circulated to the Santa Cruz Sacred Sisters.

I spent many lovely years meeting monthly with Caryn Collopy, Peggy Marketello, and Gwen Larson sharing our readings and writing. Through their help, I found my writing voice as we shared the tears and laughter of our lives. This group was inspired by Donna Love, who taught in her memoir writing class, "You don't have to start at the beginning."

Thanks to Vicki Davis, who first read my manuscript and offered insight into travel highlights. Next, Jean Maloney helped edit and support this work by offering kind advice. A big thanks goes to Nancy Hoffman for her professional editing, as well as facilitating True Tales, a monthly Scotts Valley writing group that introduced me to other inspiring writers like myself.

With gratitude to Wickepedia for historical and geographical information on various locales.

About the Author

Pamela Morgan's debut adventure memoir follows 30 years of writing legal pleadings and summaries. She considers herself a self-exploring writer, yogini, lifelong activist and earth worshiper. Pam is inspired by nature and its healing and reflective qualities. She published many short stories in the *Goddess Circle Newsletter*, for Sisters of the Sacred Circle of Santa Cruz. Her short story, "How to Love a Goddess," was published in *The Mystery of Woman*, Soul Rock Books (2012), and her story "When Santa Cruz Was Young," was published in *Santa Cruz Weird*, edited by Nancy Lynn Jarvis (2018). She resides in the Santa Cruz Redwoods with her spouse, a family of squirrels and birds, a passing Buck or Doe, and a stealthy mountain lion.

www.ingramcontent.com/pod-product-compliance
Lightning Source LLC
Chambersburg PA
CBHW031849090426
42741CB00005B/423